THE UNITED NATIONS

AND HOW IT WORKS

DAVID CUSHMAN COYLE

New Edition, with an Introduction by
Hernane Tavares de Sá
Under-Secretary for Public Information
United Nations

COLUMBIA UNIVERSITY PRESS
NEW YORK AND LONDON 1966

CONTENTS

To my wife
DORIS PORTER COYLE
with deep appreciation
for many hours of research
and for the benefit
of her judgment and editorial help
in the writing and rewriting of this book

INTRODUCTION

This book by David Cushman Coyle is now appearing in its eighth edition, revised and updated. That there has been so large a number of printings is an indication of the popularity of Mr. Coyle's "ground level" approach to telling the UN story in terms of its effect on us, or people like us.

The human side of the work of the United Nations—perhaps the most important aspect of an organization whose Charter was proclaimed in the name of the peoples of the world—is not always brought out in the day-to-day reports of its activities.

It is not a record of unvarying success. What is constant, however, is the unflagging effort to resolve for the common good problems that touch our lives at so many key points—food, shelter, livelihood, and above all, the desire to live in peace and freedom. It was recognition of these human problems and of the need for an intensified effort to help the poorer areas of the world accelerate their rate of economic and social progress that led the General Assembly of the United Nations to establish the United Nations Development Decade. This new edition of *The United Nations and How It Works* appears as the Decade of Development approaches a mid-term appraisal of its past progress and future prospects. I hope that the reader will gain from this book a better understanding of why there is need for a cooperative effort such as the Development Decade to be supported by people everywhere.

The opinions expressed in this book are, of course, the author's own, but the impression he leaves with the reader is one that most will agree parallels the thought expressed by U Thant, Secretary-General of the United Nations:

"No matter how deep the shadows may be, how sharp the conflicts, how tense the mistrust . . . we are not permitted to forget that we have too much in common, too great a sharing of interests and too much that we might lose together . . . ever to weaken our efforts to surmount the difficulties and not to turn the simple human values, which are our common heritage, into the firm foundation on which we may unite our strength and live together in peace."

Hernane Tavares de Sá
United Nations Under-Secretary for
Public Information

FOREWORD

In the spring of 1945 World War II was plainly drawing to a close. Millions of people had died in that war; millions more were homeless, hungry, and cold. The people of the whole world longed for a lasting peace. The victims of war devastation, and hundreds of millions who suffered grinding poverty even in peacetime, longed also for an escape from poverty, hunger, and disease. All over the world, too, wherever people lived under foreign domination or home-grown oppression, there was a growing demand for freedom and justice.

These deep desires for peace and for better conditions of life were joined in the great conference at San Francisco in the spring of 1945, when the nations combined their efforts in the organization of the United Nations.

The UN was organized to deal with the quarrels that might lead to war between nations. At the same time, the UN and its many working agencies have been helping the member nations in the agelong fight against human misery, injustice, and oppression.

The main purposes of the United Nations are not in conflict. It is clear that peace is necessary if the people of the world are to be free and prosperous. But peace does not come by accident; it has to be built by many kinds of action working together to provide for collective security and to remove the causes of war. United efforts to build a more prosperous world by cooperation among people of different nations and races may also help to lay the foundations for a lasting peace. People who work together against the hostile forces of nature often become friends. And finally, the united pressure of world opinion in support of human rights will in time help to reduce some of the causes of war among the peoples of the world.

The material works of the UN agencies—helping to build dams, to kill mosquitoes, to teach people to read—and its spiritual works, such as framing the Universal Declaration of Human Rights, may be fully as important for peace as the great conferences and the search for a way to control the atom.

Worldwide struggles against the hostile forces of nature are easily understood by millions of people who feel baffled by the harder problems of quarreling human nature. These material works of the UN therefore serve as a background for the UN efforts to hold the conflicts of human nature below the explosion point. The UN does not pretend that it can surely persuade or force all men to work together in harmony all the time. But it can help to bring world opinion to bear on many kinds of disputes that if left to fester between enemies might break out into deadly war.

The United Nations can talk about the rights of man, and by such talk can put moral pressure on nations where people are treated in ways that the world regards as wrong. The United Nations can take an interest in colonial peoples and in their progress toward independence or self-government—an interest that the governing powers cannot lightly brush aside.

The United Nations has been able to stop or to prevent several wars since 1945, notably in Palestine and Kashmir. In Korea the UN forces beat back the aggression. In the Congo the chaotic situation that developed in 1960 could have led to a major war but for the timely intervention of the UN. There can be, of course, no absolute guarantee that any organization on earth could surely prevent a third great war and the possible suicide of the human race. But much can be done to make that doom less likely; and much of it is being done in the United Nations.

In the United Nations, the human race is brought together, with all its virtues and faults, its wisdom and folly, and its good and ill will. This is not a world government. This is a world meeting to talk over the pressing dangers of our times and to hunt for the way to prosperity and world peace. It cannot rule the world by making and enforcing a world law with planes and atom bombs. But it can bring to bear the moral weight of world opinion. The recommendations of the Assembly of the United Nations may be all the more effective because they do not demand obedience but only ask a decent respect for the opinions of mankind.

The organization of the United Nations and how it operates are described at some length in Chapter 11. At this point it will be enough to describe briefly the main features of the UN organization.

At the center is the General Assembly, where every member nation is represented and has one vote. No nation has a veto power in the General Assembly.

The Security Council has eleven members. Five of these are the permanent members: Britain, China, France, the Union of Soviet Socialist Republics, and the United States of America. In voting on measures classed as "substantive" rather than "procedural," a motion cannot in most cases pass unless all the five permanent members vote for it. That is, each of these nations has a "veto." The difference between substantive and procedural is supposed to be related to the difference between actions on the merits of a question and actions affecting only the internal arrangements of the Council's work, but there naturally are likely to be disputes as to how a particular question is to be classified.

The six nonpermanent members of the Security Council are elected by the General Assembly for two-year terms, and do not have the veto power.

The International Court of Justice is made up of fifteen judges elected by the General Assembly and the Security Council.

The Economic and Social Council (ECOSOC) consists of the representatives of eighteen member states chosen by the General Assembly. This Council helps to coordinate the activities of many affiliated agencies dealing with international cooperation in all kinds of work, from fighting epidemics to carrying the international mails. Nongovernmental organizations are often consulted by ECOSOC on questions with which they are concerned.

Proposals for Charter amendments that would enlarge the Security Council from eleven to fifteen members and ECOSOC from eighteen to twenty-seven members have been made so that there could be room for more balanced representation of the new UN countries, mainly in Asia and Africa.

The Trusteeship Council supervises the administration of various territories that are governed by certain Powers as trustees. The Council considers reports and petitions and makes periodic visits to inspect the territories. As more and more trust territories graduate into independence the Council approaches the day of its dissolution. Many other colonial territories, because of continuous pressure from the UN, are attaining independence or self-government in free association with a nation of their own choice.

A list of the principal UN agencies, with their abbreviations, is given in Appendix A. The Charter, adopted in San Francisco in 1945 to be the Constitution of the United Nations, is given in full in Appendix B. The list of member states is given in Appendix C.

— 1 —

THE GRASS ROOTS

The United Nations headquarters in New York is a strange place where the top of the organized human race breaks through the surface. In the gallery of the Assembly you can listen to a speaker talking in a foreign tongue. Or you can put on the earphones and hear the translator giving the speech in your own language, and yet it may not sound real.

It is often real enough, however, for this is the point of contact where contending nations can grind ponderously together, striving to get what they want without the fearful costs of military war. The grinding is real, though the words themselves may seem obscure. These people are talking about something. There must be more here than meets the eye.

There is more than meets the eye. Behind the delegates are not only their nations, each with its own interests and strategy. There is also the UN itself, with its Charter and institutions, to muster the moral and material forces of mankind. The UN rests on the faith and hope of the millions of people who look to it to take their part against the danger of war and the troubles of peace. And down in the grass roots of the world, where millions of people have never learned to read or write, these people are seeing the ground-level workings of the United Nations.

Down in the grass roots the UN is building its foundations by helping people to get more to eat, and to be free of epidemic diseases, and to start hoping for a better future. The people who see that side of it soon come to understand what it means.

The Better Future

Most of the people on earth are not as well off as the people of the Western world. Children born in Southeast Asia, for instance, can expect to live about thirty years. In the United States, as of 1957, the average lifetime for men was 66.3 years and for women 72.5 years. In Norway it is several years longer. These long average lifetimes reflect comparative freedom from disease, ignorance, and poverty.

A hundred years ago the people in Western countries died young. Since then there have been changes, caused mainly by science and invention. These changes prove that many of the age-old troubles of mankind can now be reduced to small proportions or even totally abolished. All over the world those who still suffer show signs of discontent. They feel something new in the air, as if there might be an escape from their troubles, if they could only find it.

In the lands where people suffer from unnecessary ignorance, poverty, and disease, the United Nations brings a new hope. If there is time, and if the atom does not first wipe out civilization, the work of the UN among the grass roots may yet save the human race from despair.

Rice

About half the people in the world live mostly on rice. Most of the rice-eating people are poor. Rice, therefore, is a key to the main problem of survival in many overcrowded areas around the world.

Different countries have different systems for growing rice, some better than others. And there are two main kinds of rice, *japonica* and *indica*. Japonica rice in Japan yields about three times as much per acre as indica in India, but India cannot adopt japonica because it is a temperate-zone plant. The indica is suited to the tropics. This is a case for hybrids, some of which may combine the high yields of japonica with indica's ability to stand the tropical climate.

The Government of India is host to a Rice Research Scheme, sponsored by the UN Food and Agriculture Organization (FAO) and ten other Asian countries. The program has consisted of crossing varieties of japonica and indica and selecting at the different research stations the hybrids that can be used in their respective countries. No one standard hybrid can be expected to turn out best for all climates and methods of cultivation.

Several japonica-indica hybrid strains have been bred not only at the Central Rice Research Institute, Cuttack, but also in various Indian States. Some of the strains are under large-scale multiplication and distribution among the cultivators in certain areas.

As time goes on, the traditional methods of rice growing are being studied and improvements are being introduced. There are great differences in the rice yield per acre in different countries. Japan produces about 2,400 pounds of rice per acre, while the rice fields of the United States average only 1,400 pounds. Japan grows only the japonica type. In the United States japonica forms the major part of the rice crop, but small amounts of indica are also grown. In Japan, where land is scarce, more labor is put into the acre. The United States has plenty of rice land and labor is costly, so the planters use machines. They get a lower yield per acre but at a low cost per ton. Both methods are generally well suited to the conditions in which they are used, but they are not necessarily as efficient as they might become with more international exchange of information.

Farmers are slower in changing their methods of cultivation than they are in accepting new kinds of seed. This is a reason for the urgency of the hybridization project. Hybrid corn (maize) has already shown such increases over the yields of ordinary corn that it is rapidly becoming universal. In view of the great differences in yields between different strains of rice, the chances for a revolutionary improvement in most of the rice-growing countries are encouraging. Developments at the Rice Research Institute have already shown that through scientific propagation it is possible to exploit hybrid vigor in rice and thus obtain increased production.

At the present stage, the UN work in rice breeding is

unknown to the millions of people who may benefit from it. But it is not a high theory that will remain forever in the minds of learned technicians. As the new seeds are introduced the people will see the exciting change in their own lives, when the same land and the same year's labor will bring forth twice as much to eat. For people who are almost always hungry, that will seem like something to build a new world upon.

As a matter of fact, these simple grass-roots developments are usually far more profitable than ordinary business or industrial enterprises. An expenditure of half a million dollars in one of these programs can easily add a hundred million dollars' worth to the total output of a country. This is one reason why a developing country can afford to contribute most of the cost of such projects, except for what has to be paid in foreign money. As development goes on beyond the simplest improvements in agriculture and public health, the rate of return comes down to the usual commercial and industrial percentages and finance becomes a more crucial factor. But at the start, a well-managed grass-roots program can be a strong stimulus to progress not only by encouraging the people but also by giving them a quick increase of income. This is an advantage that the UN has over the old League of Nations. Forty years ago there were few chances to start such high-profit grass-roots projects, chiefly because agricultural technology was less advanced and the quick and cheap cures for the great debilitating disease had not yet been invented.

Canalboats

Canals, rivers, and lakes have always been natural highways in the flat parts of the world, and millions of people live their lives in boats on the quiet inland waterways. In East Pakistan, for instance, there are some millions of boats, from rowboats to sailing sampans, godowns —tall warehouses on rafts—and steamers and motor craft. Many of the types are ancient, and they operate with a lavish use of cheap labor. Some of the great barges are rowed with sweeps that take nine men to an oar. But progress means a rising standard of living for poor men.

No man can earn a good living pulling one-ninth of an oar. Gradually as standards and wages rise, workers must shift to more profitable jobs. Motors have to push or drag the heavy barges even on the ancient Ganges and Brahmaputra.

One of the earliest UN services in Asia came when the Government of Pakistan in 1949 turned to the United Nations for help in modernizing its inland water transport. Pakistan was not the only country with inland waterway problems, for in most of the Far East half the people live in the great river deltas and depend on water highways. One of the results of the inquiries from Asia was the organization of the Inland Water Transport Tour, an expedition of Asian experts to view the operation of waterways in other parts of the world. Members of the tour came from Burma, India, Indonesia, Pakistan, Thailand, and Vietnam. The group started by visiting Thailand, Burma, Pakistan, and India, so as to learn about one another's problems.

The Asians then proceeded to Europe, where they visited shipyards and waterways in France, Germany, and the Netherlands. They inspected new types of boats and tugs in England and Scotland. Going on to the United States, they studied traffic and equipment on the Ohio and Mississippi and along the intracoastal canals.

The members of the tour discussed the problems of water transport with experts in the countries they visited, comparing steam and diesel engines, push-towing and pull-towing, and self-propelled barges. They studied riveted and welded barges, aluminum barges, tankers and refrigerated barges, and methods of mechanical loading and unloading. The information that they collected had to be digested and sorted out to find what might be useful in Asia. The value of labor-saving in any country depends on the going rate of wages. Wages have to rise gradually as modern methods are introduced and jobs open up where the workers can earn the higher wages. If high-powered machinery is brought in too fast, it does not make the country richer. On the contrary, business is dislocated by throwing men out of work. Another limitation is the cost of foreign machinery, which has to be paid in dollars or some other foreign money. The trade balance of the country can stand just so much.

If technical improvements are introduced at the proper rate of speed, allowing time for the displaced workers to get new jobs and for the foreign-exchange costs to be covered by increased exports, progress will go along smoothly. The old League of Nations was well aware of the limitations on the proper rate of progress, and the United Nations agencies are even better aware of it. This is a part of the problem of digesting foreign information, which was one of the main jobs of the members of the Inland Water Transport Tour. They returned to their countries prepared, not to imitate what they had seen in the West, but to do their own work with a wider background of experience to stimulate their invention.

As a result many improvements have been introduced. Inland Water Transport Boards have been set up, and conferences are held regularly to stimulate progress in the equipment and management of water traffic.

Fish

Most of the people in the poorest countries are below normal in physical strength because they live almost exclusively on rice or other energy foods, with not enough protein, or body-building food. The best protein comes from animals, in the form of meat, milk, and eggs, and some of the very best kinds are found in fish. The crude methods of the past have succeeded in catching and marketing only a small fraction of the fish in the sea and in inland waters; a vast increase in the supply is possible without overfishing, provided the fisheries are scientifically managed.

If fishermen had better boats and gear, they could catch many times as much as they do, but they cannot afford better equipment nor the education and training to enable them to use it. The most practical way out of this difficulty is to form a cooperative, which will provide both the capital and the training to multiply the catch, and the processing and marketing system to bring the fish to the housewife before they spoil.

There is some sort of marketing system in most countries,

but where the traders are well enough organized to carry
the fish some distance from the coast they often have
monopoly powers that they abuse. Fishermen get too little
for their work and the consumers pay too much for their
fish. As a rule the fishermen cannot form a cooperative
without government help, especially in the poorer countries,
so the promotion of these organizations is of special interest
to the United Nations. UN institutes in various parts of the
world train executives to run cooperatives; they also train
technicians in fish processing and marketing.

In the fishing village itself, experience has shown that
the cooperative can train illiterate fishermen in a few
months to use charts, dividers, and compasses, and to
operate boats with gasoline engines and nylon nets. The
results are so profitable that even after deducting a considerable part of their catch to pay for the new equipment
they still earn two or three times as much as they had
been able to earn with the old methods. The greatly increased catch, of course, necessitates that the cooperative
provide a modern packing plant and marketing system,
and that the tributary population be persuaded to eat more
fish.

Eating more fish, where there are ancestral objections
of custom or taste, may also be a problem. Names such as
dogfish and catfish, in various languages, sometimes have
to be changed; or shark must be processed and sold as
"fillets of fish." Changed names are most easily introduced
when improved transport allows shipment of fish to new
areas where the old names are unknown.

Small technical improvements can sometimes contribute
good profits to a fishing community. Sardine fishing off
Tunis, as in other parts of the world, was traditionally
carried on at night by using a torch to attract the fish
into the net. When electric torches were invented, they
naturally were held above the water, until a UN technical
adviser invented a way of fastening the electric light below
the surface. It was found that far less electric power was
needed than in using above-water lights. The government
took up the program of equipping the fleet with under-
water fishing lights. The saving for the fleet as a whole
is estimated at nearly a million francs, or about $3,000
per night.

In Ceylon, where fishing had always been done from rafts and canoes, the government asked for an expert consultant. A Finnish naval architect, who had been a fisherman in his youth, was sent. He made friends with the Ceylonese fishermen and persuaded them to use motorboats. By 1963, Ceylon had 600 motorboats of a standard design, and they already accounted for about half the catch. A motorboat costs about $3,500, which the fisherman can borrow from the government. As he can catch about ten times as many fish as before, he can pay off the cost of the boat in about three years, and add considerably to his own income and to the food supply of the island while he is doing it.

The International Whaling Commission has decided to forbid the taking of humpback whales south of the Equator, or of blue whales in the Antarctic south of latitude 40° S. Also, the international quotas were reduced by one third. International observers travel on all factory ships.

Land Reform

In most of the countries where the farmers are poor and uneducated the ownership of farmlands is unsatisfactory. The most common source of discontent is "landlordism." The land is owned in large tracts by landlords who rent it out to the cultivators at exorbitant rents, running as high as three-fourths of the crop. The farmers naturally hate the landlords and long for the day when they themselves can own the land. The cure of these evils is not simple, and the farmers may be fooled by cruel and dishonest promises.

The most obvious way for enraged farmers to get rid of their rent burdens might seem to be to liquidate the landlords and take over the land. The drawback is that such violent methods would not protect the farmers from the kind of government that would go with them. After the farmer got possession of his land, he might find that the taxes, the forced deliveries to the government, and the days of forced labor on government work, would add up to a heavier burden than before.

The UN had a Conference on Natural Resources in 1949, where most of the delegates crowded into the meetings on land reform. They discussed the problems of their various countries and learned how complex the subject can be.

The General Assembly therefore passed a resolution in 1950 asking the Secretary-General and the FAO to study the problems of landholding. In 1951 the Economic and Social Council discussed the Secretary-General's report, and recommended to the member governments that they take up land reform "in the interest of the landless, small, and medium farmers." The United States sponsored a World Conference, and many countries started programs to improve the conditions of landownership.

One of the most successful land distribution programs so far has been in Japan, where the Occupation authorities directed the purchase of five million acres from landlords. The land was sold to the tenants at fair prices and the payments were spread over thirty years with an interest rate of only 3.2 percent. The farmers had a good bargain and they knew it. An important feature of the Japanese program was management by local land committees.

Dr. Bennett, the late head of the United States Point Four Program, offered the following general principles for a just and equitable agricultural system:

First, the farmer must be able to own land, or to use the land he tills under fair conditions and terms of tenure. Second, the farmer must have access to credit on reasonable terms to enable him to farm efficiently, whether as owner or tenant. Third, he must have access to knowledge and techniques that will make his efforts productive and profitable to him and to society.

Techniques have been developed through which the success of the farmer on his land can be hastened and rendered more secure. The system of "supervised credit," for instance, offers the farmer enough credit to buy machinery, fertilizer, and high-grade seed, on his agreement to follow a plan of operations worked out with a technical adviser. Ordinarily the result is an increase in production and income that appears almost miraculous.

The Economic and Social Council in 1957 suggested

that governments undertake studies of the effects of land-reform measures on production, living standards, and economic and social development. It also called attention to the fact that technical advice could be obtained from the UN and various specialized agencies.

In 1958 the Council suggested the establishment of regional research and training centers to study problems of land tenure and land use and invited FAO and other appropriate agencies to cooperate in this work.

The Agencies

The UN work at the grass roots is carried on by several agencies that deal with the basic material enemies of man—hunger, disease, and poverty.

Hunger is the special problem of the Food and Agriculture Organization (FAO), which was started in 1943 at a conference of national representatives in Hot Springs, Virginia. FAO has its own constitution and membership; not all FAO members belong to the UN. It has its own income derived from dues paid by the members, and its own governing body, the FAO Conference, which meets every two years. FAO is one of the specialized agencies affiliated with the UN through an agreement with the Economic and Social Council, approved by the UN General Assembly.

FAO sends experts to help countries that want technical advice on how to grow more food and other crops, how to control pests and plant and animal diseases, how to protect food in storage, and in general how to increase the yield of farms, fisheries, and forests.

FAO advises on soil conservation and the use of fertilizers. It provides fellowships for technicians to study in foreign countries where they can learn techniques that they can use at home. It also publishes technical yearbooks and other material useful in agriculture, forestry, and fisheries.

FAO is cooperating with other UN agencies to promote economic development in many parts of the world. As a rule, unless a country has rich oil fields, its agricultural program is a vitally important part of its economic development. Usually more than half its workers are on the farms;

their efficiency must be raised so that many of them can leave the farm and take jobs in factories or service enterprises.

Although a traveler in an underdeveloped country may easily get the impression that farming is still entirely primitive, the statistics indicate that since the founding of FAO the rate of agricultural production in these countries has risen notably. Production in the Far East, for instance, increased 35 percent during the ten years from 1950 to 1960, or a little faster than the growth of population. This compares favorably with agricultural progress during the developmental period in England. Wheat yields in England increased only 30 percent from 1750 to 1850, or less than one-tenth as fast as the growth of agricultural yields under modern conditions of development.

In a modern development campaign, agricultural progress does more than simply release manpower for growing industry. It also provides food for export or as a substitute for imported food, thus freeing foreign exchange for the purchase of machinery and other foreign goods needed for growth. It may also help to improve the quality of the food supply, which is usually deficient in meat, fruits, and vegetables. These additions to a balanced diet will do much to improve the people's health, ability to work, and capacity to learn.

To carry on its work, FAO has ten principal divisions, including Land and Water Development, Plant Production and Protection, Animal Production and Health, Forestry, Fisheries, Nutrition, and various economic branches. It works closely with other UN and regional agencies, such as those of the Organization of American States.

In recent years FAO has been especially interested in the terms of trade in agricultural products, since many of the less-developed countries depend on agricultural exports, which have been falling in price on the world markets since the end of the Korean War. Another aspect of trade that has claimed the urgent attention of FAO is the use of agricultural surpluses from the United States and other advanced countries to help in development programs. Countries that are short of food can use these surplus supplies to save the cost of food imports, reduce inflation of domestic food prices, and improve the health of workers.

To focus the widespread work of FAO, the Director-General of the Organization in July, 1960, launched a five-year Freedom-from-Hunger Campaign. The campaign emphasizes educational programs, research and technical advances, and action programs in various countries to demonstrate new methods.

FAO illustrates an important difference between the League of Nations technical agencies and those of the United Nations. A technical agency commonly does three kinds of work: (1) It is a clearinghouse of scientific information through which technical papers are exchanged among scientists of member nations. (2) It promotes standardized legal arrangements among the nations in connection with its specialty. Both these types of work were done by the League agencies and are now carried on by those connected with the UN. (3) It provides technical assistance, of which there was almost none under the League.

Since it is technical assistance that brings the UN into direct contact with millions of people, this difference from the old League is important. In this respect the UN has broader foundations than the League; this may make the difference between life and death for the UN.

World Health Organization (WHO)

The World Health Organization was started by a conference in New York in July, 1946, where representatives of sixty-one countries set up an Interim Commission to work on international health. The permanent organization came into being on April 7, 1948, when twenty-six members had ratified its constitution. April 7 is now celebrated all over the world as World Health Day.

Even before 1948 the Interim Commission had begun to show what an international organization could do. Egypt was suddenly attacked by an epidemic of cholera in September, 1947. The Commission straightway mustered the cholera experts of the world, and the necessary materials for them to work with. By the end of December the epidemic was wiped out.

WHO is a specialized agency which advises member countries on public health and the control of disease. It makes war on the widespread plagues such as malaria, tuberculosis, yaws, and syphilis, and on less common diseases including leprosy, typhus, polio, diphtheria, and bilharziasis, or snail fever, which is carried by water snails that live in irrigation ditches.

In 1955 WHO undertook a worldwide campaign to wipe malaria from the face of the earth, a campaign that has been called "the greatest challenge in the history of humanity's fight for health." One of the most important discoveries of this century is the simple fact that a mosquito that has bitten a malaria patient will rest on the nearest wall to digest the meal, so if the inside walls of the houses are sprayed with DDT, the infected mosquitoes will get it on their feet and die before they can go out and infect another victim.

Unfortunately, insect poisons such as DDT do not work forever; the insects develop an immunity. A few individual insects are able to survive the poison, and they live to lay eggs. After a few generations the number of immune insects becomes so great that the poison is no longer effective, and a new one has to be adopted. Meanwhile the heavy use of chemical poisons will tend to kill off useful insects such as bees, as well as birds, animals, and even people.

Since the antimalaria campaign depends on killing insects, haste is important; the hope is to eliminate malaria completely from as many areas as possible before the mosquitoes win the battle against the poisons. Thereafter, if a malaria case moves into a clean area, he must be kept under screens, where no mosquito can reach him until he is no longer infectious.

In the Western Pacific area, for instance, malaria has been practically eliminated from Taiwan and the Ryukyu Islands, and is expected to be extinct by 1969 in North Borneo, Sarawak, Brunei, and the Philippines.

Europe is now reported to be entirely free of new malaria cases, except for such as may occasionally come in after being infected elsewhere.

WHO manages the worldwide quarantine regulations established in 1951 to replace other agreements dating back as far as 1903. WHO in Geneva receives an average of eight to ten telegrams every day, reporting cases of the quarantinable diseases—cholera, plague, relapsing fever, typhus, smallpox, or yellow fever. This information is sent out daily by radio and weekly in printed form in the *Epidemiological Record*. WHO also sends out information on other diseases that may spread rapidly around the world, such as influenza.

Even in Europe, where most of the member nations are industrialized and highly developed, WHO is not without health problems in which it can help to coordinate the work of its member countries. Such problems include the diseases of old age, such as heart troubles, and the effects of over-industrialization, such as air pollution and mental disorders.

On the other hand, in the countries around the Eastern end of the Mediterranean WHO still has to fight the ancient plagues of leprosy, malaria, trachoma, tuberculosis, and various waterborne diseases that kill great numbers of children and cut down the working capacity of grown people.

The most important obstacle to rapid improvement of world health is the scarcity of trained medical and public health workers. Doctors, for instance, are scarce in the underdeveloped countries where conditions are worst. In highly advanced countries there may be 500 people to one doctor, but in others there are 50,000 or more to one doctor. WHO therefore spends a large part of its money on the encouragement of medical education. In 1962, WHO granted more than 1,700 fellowships to qualified health workers of various kinds for study abroad. It also encourages the erection of teaching institutions for health workers, and supplies professors to help them in starting their work.

WHO is active in coordinating the many lines of medical research that are being pursued in various parts of the world. It is especially interested in promoting cancer research, investigating such matters as the effects of tobacco and other kinds of smoke, mass chewing of betel nut, and various food additives. To promote the exchange of cancer information this world organization has established centers where specimens are classified and from which samples are sent to other centers. Enough progress in the prevention and cure of cancers has been made to give hope for further advances, and the worldwide exchange of knowledge, promoted by WHO, will hasten this process.

The same may be said of the detection and prohibition of new drugs that turn out to have disastrous side effects, such as producing defective babies. WHO acts as a clearing-house for information on dangerous drugs, and also supplies samples of standardized antibiotics and other pharmaceuticals to be used in testing the strength of such preparations.

International Labor Organization (ILO)

Another agency that often works in close contact with great numbers of people is the International Labor Organization. ILO was founded in 1919 as a self-governing institution affiliated with the League of Nations. It is now a specialized agency associated with the UN.

The annual Conference of the ILO promotes laws for the protection of wage earners by proposing international agreements which the delegates are obligated to take home and submit to their governments for ratification. A government that ratifies one of these agreements binds itself to report each year on what progress it is making toward passing the laws called for in the agreement. From 1919 to June, 1964, ILO adopted 119 agreements and received notice of nearly 3,000 ratifications.

The ILO works in many ways to promote social justice for workers around the world. Among its projects are vocational training and workers' education programs in the less-developed countries. It offers assistance to cooperatives and small-scale industry. Since 1956 ILO has been studying the effects of automation and other advanced forms of technology, and is prepared to offer help to both the developing and the advanced nations in seeking ways to overcome the dislocating effects on labor that follow the introduction of these methods. ILO has set up an International Institute for Labor Studies, which provides training for government officials, management, and labor-union officers to help them meet their responsibilities in this field.

UNICEF

The United Nations International Children's Emergency Fund (UNICEF) was created by the General Assembly in 1946. UNRRA, the UN Relief and Rehabilitation Administration, which had been set up to relieve victims of war devastation, was closing its work in 1946, and UNICEF took over the relief of children who still needed help. UNICEF is not supported by the UN budget, but by voluntary contributions from governments and individuals —including the sale of the widely used UNICEF Christmas cards.

By 1950 the war devastation had been largely repaired, and UNICEF turned its main attention to the children in underdeveloped countries. Of the thousand million children in the world, about 750 million are in the less-developed countries. At least one in every five of these children will die before reaching the age of five, and two-thirds of them are seriously exposed to ignorance, hunger, and disease.

Two of the most important jobs at UNICEF have been its campaigns against yaws and tuberculosis.

Yaws is a disease of hot, damp climates. Yaws makes masses of open sores. It is extremely contagious, and especially afflicts children. Few die of yaws, but many become helpless cripples and a lifelong burden on their relatives.

Yaws can be cured with one dose of penicillin costing less than three cents.

Tuberculosis is another mass plague that strikes most often where living conditions are poor, and most often strikes children and young people. In India, for instance, TB kills about half a million people a year. It is also a great cause of poverty because it is a slow killer. People waste away and cannot work to support themselves.

In the crowded countries with low standards of living, there is no present chance to send the TB patients to hospitals for treatment. But there is one thing that can be done quickly, and that is to vaccinate the children who have not yet caught the disease.

The vaccine, known as BCG, discovered in France fifty years ago, has been developed and tested on a large scale by the Scandinavians. In 1948 UNICEF and the Scandinavians joined forces with WHO to put on campaigns in countries that asked for help.

The BCG teams go into a village and test the children for TB. Those who have not been infected are vaccinated. Of those who are vaccinated, about 80 percent cannot get TB for four or five years, and the other 20 percent will not have it severely. From then on it is necessary only to vaccinate all newborn babies and keep up the immunity of the others. As the unfortunate ones who were already infected gradually die off, the number of cases and the amount of infection will diminish. Finally, if the country grows rich enough, and if the search for still newer drugs proceeds as expected, the disease can be virtually wiped out.

In the meantime, the operation is extremely profitable. One vaccination costs only a few cents. The child who doesn't get TB may grow up and earn his own living instead of being a burden on his family. For a few cents every four years, the profit to the country is high.

In 1952 UNICEF and WHO launched an experimental campaign against trachoma in Morocco. Trachoma is an eye disease that often causes blindness. Some good results were obtained, but it was evident that a massive attack on the universal plague of flies would be needed, since flies carry the disease. That in turn must depend on widespread health education.

In 1953, when the International Children's Emergency Fund came to the end of its emergency charter, the Fund reported that it had vaccinated 22 million children with BCG, cured 3 million of yaws, protected 12 million from malaria, and so on through a long list. The General Assembly voted unanimously to continue the Fund indefinitely and gave it a new name, the UN Children's Fund. But the initials UNICEF were kept as a trademark. To millions of people, the only United Nations they know is UNICEF, the friend of children.

By 1964 UNICEF reported that in place of about 200 million people formerly threatened with yaws, there were only 100 million still living in yaws territory, and that 162 million children had been vaccinated with BCG supplied by UNICEF. Millions more were being protected against trachoma and against leprosy.

More than half the children born each year come into the world without benefit of any trained attendance. UNICEF has helped equip more than 26,000 health centers, where village midwives are taught basic rules of hygiene and where mothers may come for help and advice before and after the birth of their children.

In the developing countries there is a widespread lack of proper food for children, especially protein foods and milk. UNICEF provides imported machinery for milk pasteurization; hatchery fish for stocking fishponds; vegetable garden seeds; poultry; and equipment for making new foods such as soya and peanut flour, and fish-protein concentrate.

Rapid social and economic changes in the developing countries unavoidably lead to the disruption of traditional habits of family and village life. To help meet this situation UNICEF supports special programs to improve the care given to children in their own homes or in day centers. Homemaking and improved methods of rearing children are taught through women's clubs and community development organizations.

In recent years UNICEF has devoted more and more effort to the education and training of adults for work connected with the welfare of children, as well as to schools for the children themselves. It helps to support the training of teachers, to improve school courses, and to set up vocational training for older children.

UNICEF specializes in the furnishing of supplies, equipment, and vehicles, most of which must come from outside the country where UNICEF is working. The host country provides most of the workers and supplies that do not have to be imported—which together amount to a large part of the cost of the work. These payments amount to about 2½ times as much as is spent by UNICEF. In 1963 UNICEF allotted about 10 million dollars to support projects in over one hundred countries. Much of the UNICEF work is done in cooperation with WHO and FAO.

Other Agencies

The other principal UN agency working directly at the grass roots is the UN Educational, Scientific, and Cultural Organization (UNESCO), which covers the whole field of education and therefore overlaps all the other agencies. It is entitled to a separate chapter and is described in Chapter 2.

Several important programs aiding the underdeveloped countries to raise their standards of living are being carried on outside the UN. One is the AID Program of the United States; another is the Colombo Plan set up by members of the British Commonwealth. There are also numerous private institutions working on special problems, such as the Rockefeller Foundation and the Ford Foundation. The Organization of American States has many specialized agencies for development work, often in close cooperation with the UN agencies. France and the Soviet Union have widespread programs for aiding economic development in various parts of the world.

When the UN agencies are asked to assist a country with technical development, they request the government to arrange that all organizations related to the proposed work be brought into a cooperative plan. An example is the rehabilitation center for cripples at Solo in Java, started by an Indonesian surgeon after the war. In 1954 the UN sent an expert from the United States to visit Solo. As a result of his report the center was built up with the cooperative help of the Indonesian Government, the United Nations, the World Veteran's Foundation, ILO, WHO, and the Directors of the Colombo Plan.

Material and Moral

What does growing more rice have to do with saving the world from destruction by the H-bomb? Isn't this just playing with pebbles on the beach while an earthquake is sending a tidal wave to wash us all away? It is a dangerous world but it is not as simple as that.

The United Nations has to save the world, if possible, from the H-bomb in the next few years and from more and worse in the future, from now on as long as civilization endures. In the long run, the human race may survive if people learn not to fear and distrust one another as much as they do now. Organizations to deter military aggression and to build up a secure and harmonious world are necessary. But underlying all that, the issue of life or death is moral, not only among the delegates who discuss and argue in the great conferences but also among the people at home.

When the United Nations sends a team of foreign experts into a village to cure disease or to increase the food supply, they are expected to train local people and work with them. The local contribution to each project is generally many times as large as that of the UN, in terms of labor, equipment, and money. The material purpose of the work is a necessary part of the moral relation that is created among these people. Being a material thing, the reduction of disease or the increase of food can be seen and agreed upon. In the simplest kinds of "development" there is no argument. The people unite to create a new thing and see that it is good. They can shake hands and feel the bond of friendship in a successful common adventure. This is the most fundamental way that goodwill can come among men of different races, religions, and cultures.

But almost the same kind of activity can create hatreds. When men work together as master and slave, or as conqueror and subject people, without mutual respect or a common purpose, they can build deep-seated hatreds. There are such hatreds today in most of the world.

When any sort of "project" is undertaken, therefore, the question has to arise: Is someone out to exploit the workers in this project for some purpose that they do not think is good? Is this development program a trap to get political control of the country? Or are the foreigners trying to make friends in order to win allies in a war they are planning? Or do the foreigners simply hope to make a commercial profit out of the country's development? If the foreigners have enemies, the enemies will tell the people that the development projects are a trap. In the long run the people are going to judge the honesty of the foreign experts who offer to help them, and they will give them friendship or hatred accordingly.

There is no dishonesty in wanting to do business with a growing and prosperous country, if it is honest business with profit to all concerned in it. There is no dishonesty in wanting to make friends in order to have allies for the defense of peace, if the real plan is to defend peace and not to start an aggressive war. Selfish reasons for helping in an enterprise are not wrong if they are reasons that everyone agrees are good.

In fact, good hardheaded reasons for taking part in a development project are valuable because they are easier to believe than a professed love of doing good for its own sake. The foreigners, especially, do well to hunt for hard, well-understood reasons by which to explain themselves in order to ward off the natural suspicion with which many people often regard strangers.

It is natural for an engineer to get satisfaction from seeing the plans of his brain take form in a stout bridge that is praised by the people who needed a bridge. It is natural for a doctor to enjoy winning a tough battle against a disease. Under the UN flag, men can go on a mission with men of other nations to do a job that plainly gives them these creative satisfactions. The same satisfactions are, to be sure, common among the technicians who work for the United States AID Program or the Colombo Plan, or for one of the private foundations. But in places where the people are keenly suspicious of the Great Powers, the same technicians can go under UN auspices and be more readily accepted.

The best of all reasons for technical cooperation is that, carried through in the spirit of good will, it builds the foundations of peace as well as prosperity. At the grass roots of the world, the people may be ignorant of books, but they are wise in human nature. They are suspicious of charity, but they do not miss the meaning of these simple village improvements. In the long run, if the human race is so fortunate as to have a long run, these foundations will bear the growing structure of good will among men.

It is particularly valuable to demonstrate that all the nations can contribute to the pool of knowledge. When, for instance, an expert to fight livestock diseases was needed in Tunisia, one was sent from Ceylon. Colombia has provided a radio specialist for Pakistan. Icelandic fisheries experts have helped to modernize the fishing industries of Ceylon, India, and Turkey. In 1956 India contributed eighty-nine experts for service abroad. The worldwide mutual respect on which peace must finally rest is built up by all such interchanges through which nations that are giving help are also receiving help from others. This growing network of knowledge, with the network of good will which, in the best conditions, grows with it, cannot solve all the fearful problems of a world threatened with destruction, but they are a necessary part of the solution.

The improvement in living conditions where technical assistance has been given by the UN or by the various national and private programs has been notable in many localities and in some places even spectacular. But it is important to remember that so far only scattered lamps of progress have been lighted in a vast gray landscape. This slow total progress is only partially caused by lack of money. Even more it is the effect of scarcity of experts qualified to teach and learn and also free to move to foreign lands. More rapid progress has to depend not only on more generous contributions of money but also on training more persons to do the work.

EDUCATION, SCIENCE, AND CULTURE

When the DDT team has left the village and the mosquitoes and bugs are, for the time being, dead, then what is going to happen? The people will sleep better of nights, and before long they will notice that fewer people have chills and fever. But will they then join enthusiastically in the march of progress, or will they go on with their ancient customs, merely hoping that some day the spray team may come back and clean up the bugs for them again?

Most people, and especially those who cannot read, are conservative in their ways. They may have heard of the wonders of progress, and may have seen a few of the magic tricks of science. But they do not quickly see how many of their ancestral customs they would have to change if they want to enter the new world where such tricks are done.

It is not even enough to learn to drive a jeep. Someone has to know how to worry about unusual noises in its interior. It is not enough to be rid for a while of the large visible insects that can be killed by DDT. Someone has to learn to worry about dirt and deadly creatures that are invisible. And that is only the beginning. The higher the standard of living rises, the more things have to be attended to and the more the people have to know in order to make the system work.

Education, therefore, is a special requirement that has to be supplied with all the other kinds of development in agriculture, health, industry, or political-economic institu-

tions. Not only must the people who will do the work,
from vaccinating to banking, be trained for their jobs, but
the whole population has to be educated to believe in
progress and to accept necessary changes without too much
delay. This necessity for keeping all parts of the procession
coming along is a common source of trouble in even the
advanced nations. As the less-developed nations hurry to
take on the methods of modern science, there will be the
same kind of troubles. Parts of the social and political
system will be slow to develop the new qualities that are
necessary to make the new projects work successfully.

The UN Educational, Scientific, and Cultural Organization, known as UNESCO, grew out of conferences among
the governments in exile in London during the last years of
World War II. The Nazi invasion of western Europe in
1940 had destroyed a large part of the educational system
of the conquered countries. The governments of those
countries knew that after liberation their schools and
universities would need books and equipment, new buildings, and new teachers to replace those who could not be
found. So a Conference of Allied Ministers of Education
was formed in London to study reports of damage and to
look for means of restoration as soon as their countries
should be liberated.

In the meantime the Allies began planning for a United
Nations Organization, and it was evident that the new
organization would have to take an interest in education
all over the world. The London Conference of Allied
Ministers began to invite representatives from other countries outside of Europe. The United States sent a delegation
to the Conference in April, 1944.

The United States belief in mutual understanding as a
means of building friendship and peace has deep roots
in tradition. For instance, in 1859 Abraham Lincoln told
a farmers' meeting:

> From the first appearance of man upon the earth
> down to very recent times, the words "stranger"
> and "enemy" were quite or almost synonymous. . . .
> Even yet, this has not totally disappeared. The man of
> the highest moral cultivation, in spite of all which
> abstract principle can do, likes him whom he does

know much better than him whom he does not know. To correct the evils, great and small, which spring from want of sympathy, and from positive enmity among strangers, as nations or as individuals, is one of the highest functions of civilization.*

The need for wide international contacts in education, science, and culture was clear to the delegates from all over the world at San Francisco. The UN Charter authorized the UN to promote the formation of an affiliated agency for educational and cultural development. A conference for that purpose met in London in November, 1945, and wrote a constitution for the United Nations Educational, Scientific, and Cultural Organization which was signed on November 16, 1945.

UNESCO exists in its own right by virtue of the fact that its members have accepted its constitution. Its members are not necessarily members of the UN. Its regular revenue does not come from the UN, but from the direct contributions of its member nations. The organization's General Conference, meeting once every two years, adopts its budget and assesses the contributions from the members. The routine management is carried on by an executive board of thirty members.

The Need for Education

Nearly half of the world's children have no schooling whatever. As the population of the world increases by about 50 million people a year, UNESCO estimates that the number of grown people unable to read or write is increasing by at least 20 million a year. Altogether, there are now about 700 million illiterate adults in the world.

Meanwhile the demand for economic and social modernization has spread around the world; but modernization, after the first few simple stages, cannot go far among people who cannot read. There is, accordingly, a rising pressure for education.

For countries with limited resources the problem of

* Address to Wisconsin State Agricultural Society, Milwaukee, September 30, 1859.

whom to educate first may be a hard one to face. Shall the government neglect some of its children in order to concentrate on training the engineers it desperately needs? The best answer is likely to be different in every case. In 1963 UNESCO established an International Institute for Educational Planning in Paris, with the help of the World Bank and the Ford Foundation, to help solve the problems of setting up properly balanced educational programs. The Institute has sent planning missions to most of the developing countries, and offers training for school administrators and planners from Asia, Africa, and Latin America.

In 1957 UNESCO began promoting regional surveys of the overwhelming problems of providing teachers and schoolrooms for millions of children. Representatives of the Latin-American Republics met and decided to emphasize the extension of primary education over a ten-year period. UNESCO helped them by training statisticians and school administrators, by setting up pilot teacher-training institutes, and by providing expert missions to guide the project. With the help of UNICEF, UNESCO is now setting up centers to train primary-school teachers in the most modern classroom methods.

Since 1957, the Latin-American countries have trained 90,000 teachers and established places for 4,000,000 more children in schools. In addition, with UNESCO help, the subjects taught have been tailored to meet current needs and the region is on the way toward a goal promised since the 1850's—six years of free schooling for all.

In Africa the problem is more serious. Adult illiteracy in many countries is between 80 and 85 percent. As for higher education, only two children out of a thousand have a chance to go to college. At the time of the Congo crisis in 1960, there were only seventeen Congolese college graduates in the entire country. It is not surprising, then, that African educators are giving priority to the expansion of secondary schools and vocational training. Without people to run the waterworks, banks, educational ministries, and the many other organizations required by a modern nation, these states would face collapse.

With the help of the United Nations Special Fund, UNESCO has set up thirteen secondary-school teacher-training colleges, which will soon be turning out more than

1,800 high-school teachers a year. In addition, UNESCO has set up textbook centers and a school building center to guide the African nations in supplying these necessities. Half of the 130 million children in Asia do not go to school. To educate these children by 1980 would cost 56,000 million dollars. At the same time, these Asian countries desperately need trained technicians if they are to climb quickly into the twentieth century.

UNESCO helps governments plan expanded educational programs, budget the necessary funds, and set up the required training and research institutions. An example is the Teachers College at Ubol, Thailand, some 140 miles east of Bangkok. The college is a joint enterprise of UNESCO and the Government of Thailand. Starting with 175 boys and girls and 18 teachers, eight years later it had grown to over one thousand students. The teaching staff includes a number of United States Peace Corps volunteers. In addition to the usual subjects the students learn how to teach young people to raise poultry and pigs, how to raise more fish in the ponds, and how to weave mats and handbags. They also learn how to work with the older people. As a result, many farmers who used to raise only one crop of rice, taking five months out of the year, now utilize the other seven months to raise a crop of cotton, coffee, jute, or a second crop of rice.

There are now twenty-four similar teacher-training colleges scattered all over the country.

All around the world, UNESCO has helped to establish eighteen engineering and scientific institutes. It reports that many of the schools are as large as the Massachusetts Institute of Technology, and offer an equally wide range of courses.

Campaign for Universal Literacy

UNESCO estimates that the problem of illiteracy could be wiped out if the developed countries would contribute the equivalent of about fifteen cents a year per head of their populations for a period of ten years. In 1963 the General Assembly called on UNESCO to study the feasibility of such a campaign.

In the last years of the 1960's UNESCO will launch

pilot projects in eight countries to work out the best methods for a mass campaign. It will study how to provide reading materials that will be useful to the people and also interesting to read, since adults who learn to read and do not use their new skill will lose it in a few weeks.

In some countries there are no popular reading materials in the languages spoken by the people. UNESCO is helping eight Asian countries to organize the production, publication, and distribution of desirable books. A regional center has been in operation in Karachi since 1955, serving not only Pakistan but Burma, Ceylon, India, and Iran. In 1963 this service was extended to Afghanistan, Nepal, and Thailand. UNESCO also plans to encourage the establishment of local newspapers, seven of which have already been founded in Ghana with UNESCO help.

Public libraries have been opened in New Delhi, in Nigeria, and in Colombia, and have proved highly popular, especially with young people and children. The use of bookmobiles—another method for supplying the people with good reading matter—will no doubt be widely extended in the further development of the literacy program.

By 1970 UNESCO hopes to be in a position to launch its worldwide literacy campaign as an essential part of the modernization movement that is beginning to sweep around the world.

Science

In the developed countries UNESCO plays its part by sponsoring scientific conventions, over one hundred of them every year, where scientists from all over the world meet to discuss their various specialties, ranging from cell biology and brain research to the design and use of electronic computers. One such meeting resulted in the establishment of the European Center for Nuclear Research, which has grown to such a size that it now has a larger budget than UNESCO.

UNESCO helped to organize the International Geophysical Year (1957–58), and is a sponsor of the program of study called the "Years of the Quiet Sun," during which scientists will measure the sun's activities during the periods when its magnetic storms and sunspots are at their lowest ebb.

The largest ocean survey ever undertaken, the International Indian Ocean Expedition, was launched under UNESCO auspices in 1962. It is operated by the Inter-governmental Oceanographic Commission. Forty ships from twenty nations are making a systematic study of the Indian Ocean, which was previously little known. Mapping the mountains and canyons of the ocean floor is only the beginning. Other types of information are collected by marine biologists, geophysicists, chemists, and meteorologists. The results are studied at centers in Washington and Moscow, and information about fish populations, ocean currents, and probable weather conditions is supplied to interested nations.

The Commission is also undertaking research projects in the Atlantic and off the coast of Japan.

One direct practical advantage of these ocean research programs is that fisheries will be able to increase their catch without overexploiting the resource. This increase will be especially beneficial in Southeast Asia, where the populations suffer from lack of sufficient protein in their food supply. Other practical benefits may include the dredging of minerals from the ocean floor and the separation of valuable chemicals from seawater.

Since 1957 UNESCO has been promoting research on the problems of arid zones, which comprise about one-third of the land surface of the earth. These studies will reach a climax in the International Hydrological Decade, beginning in 1965. Scientists throughout the world will cooperate in mapping underground water and in designing ways to increase the available supplies. In the summer of 1964 the U.S. Government joined with UNESCO to sponsor a one-week conference on the desalting of sea-water and other salty waters.

Another branch of science that UNESCO is promoting is seismology, or the study of earthquakes. Through a special institute in Tokyo, UNESCO is helping to train a generation of seismologists who in time may develop methods for more definite prediction of probable earthquakes. The engineering technology for building earthquake-proof structures is already well developed, but needs to be more widely adopted in countries where earthquakes are possible.

Social Sciences and Culture

In 1963 UNESCO published the first volume of a six-volume *Cultural and Scientific History of Mankind,* written and edited by many experts from various member states. The impartial character of this work has met with wide acclaim from scholars and the public alike.

A principal aim of UNESCO is to develop understanding and goodwill among widely differing nations and peoples. It has pioneered, for instance, in the study of race and race relations as seen from the social, scientific, and religious points of view. One important recent study examines methods by which young people whose parents will allow such teaching can be taught to avoid race-hatred and to respect other races. In an important sense, all the grass-roots programs of the UN agencies help to lay foundations for friendly relations among differing races and cultures.

Since 1957 UNESCO has been carrying on a campaign to promote better understanding between Eastern and Western cultures by arranging for translations of their literary masterpieces into each other's languages, by the exchange of scholars and artists, and by traveling exhibitions and theatrical performances.

Another important aspect of this work is that authors are encouraged to avoid expressions of national prejudice in writing of other countries and peoples. Many countries already exchange textbooks—a good method for ensuring greater objectivity and a more realistic view of the world.

UNESCO is taking a leading part in the efforts to save from destruction the many cultural treasures of the Nile Valley that are threatened by the rising waters behind the great Aswan Dam. By 1964 some fourteen national archeological teams had been at work seeking out and rescuing important relics in the area. Many ancient temples and Christian churches had been moved to safe ground. A cofferdam had been built around Abu Simbel, the great temples of Pharaoh Rameses II and his Queen, carved more than 3,000 years ago from the living rock. While the cofferdam holds back the rising waters, the archeological surgeons will cut the colossal statues with electronically-guided saws into thirty-ton blocks, which will then be reassembled at a new site beyond the reach of the waters.

UNESCO has proposed an international agreement protecting the copyright on literary works, which by 1964 had been signed by forty-seven countries, and another protecting broadcasters, performers, and recording companies, signed by twenty-five countries. The Free-Flow agreement, for duty-free circulation of educational and information materials, had been accepted by forty-four countries, and forty-nine had adhered to the Convention on the protection of cultural properties in case of war.

A UNESCO survey completed in 1962 indicated that about 70 percent of the human race has no reasonably good source of information about events outside the village. UNESCO is therefore encouraging the spread of national news services, and has sponsored advanced journalistic studies in two countries, France and Ecuador. It is also studying new developments such as communications satellites, and in Africa is helping with the establishment of a TV network.

Coupons

In the first years after World War II, UNESCO promoted the supply of books and educational equipment for countries where dollars were scarce, by issuing international coupons to educators in those countries, which could be used for purchases in the United States and other "hard-currency" nations. By 1964 this program had moved material to a total value of over $60,000,000.

The coupon scheme was so successful that another plan was added. Gift coupons are for sale in Argentina, Australia, Belgium, Canada, Denmark, the Federal Republic of Germany, Finland, France, Israel, Italy, Japan, the Netherlands, New Zealand, Norway, Sweden, Switzerland, the United Kingdom, and the United States. Private persons and organizations in these countries may choose a Project from a UNESCO catalog of Gift Projects. The donor buys UNESCO coupons and sends them to the Project. The Project can then use the coupons as a kind of money order in the currency of the country from which they came. An additional advantage of this system is that it may help to set up contacts between people in different countries who are interested in education.

Still another coupon scheme provides help for students to travel in foreign countries where they need foreign money for expenses. These coupons are intended mainly for people from soft-currency countries who cannot convert their money into the currency of the countries where they plan to go.

National Commissions

The UNESCO Constitution provides that each member state shall make arrangements for bringing its educational, scientific, and cultural organizations in touch with UNESCO, preferably by forming a national commission.

In the United States, for example, a National Commission for UNESCO was established by an Act of Congress. About eighty private organizations, ranging from the American Association for the Advancement of Science and the American Farm Bureau Federation, to the Congress of Industrial Organizations, the Negro Newspaper Publishers Association, and the U.S. Junior Chamber of Commerce, are affiliated with the National Commission. The one hundred Commission members are appointed by the Secretary of State. The affiliated organizations nominate sixty members; most of the others come from federal, state, and local government. The Commission helps the government in its relations with UNESCO; it helps in recruiting experts for UNESCO missions and suitable delegates for UNESCO conferences. It holds a national conference every other year, and publishes material on UNESCO that it regards as useful for the information of the people of the United States.

UNESCO has been criticized by people hostile to the United Nations, especially by some of those in the United States who are known as "isolationists." In order to determine whether there was any substance to such attacks, in 1953 President Eisenhower appointed a committee of three distinguished citizens to study UNESCO activities. The committee reported that UNESCO does not advocate world government or world citizenship in the political sense, does not try to undermine national loyalties, does not interfere with the United States school system, and does not show any evidence of atheism or hostility toward religion.

The many-sided work of UNESCO represents a part of the many-sided life of the human race. It represents the healthy peacetime interests of people all over the world. It helps to build up the sane side of human life, in the hope that the sane part of the human mind will in time get the better of the part that falls into war.

— 3 —

MONEY AND TRADE

International prosperity depends partly on production, partly on the exchange of the money of different countries, and partly on the conditions for exchanging goods and services. The UN has many agencies helping with production, one of which is the International Bank for Reconstruction and Development, which promotes international investment. The International Monetary Fund helps to smooth the exchange of currencies, and the General Agreement on Tariffs and Trade serves as a bargaining market where nations can make agreements to reduce tariffs and other trade barriers.

The World Bank

The International Bank was organized at a conference at Bretton Woods, New Hampshire, U.S.A., in the summer of 1944 along with its sister institution, the Monetary Fund. By 1963 the bank had 101 member nations.

At the start the authorized capital of the Bank was 10,000 million dollars. Each member nation subscribed to the stock of the Bank for an amount based in general on its wealth and trade, varying from $3,175,000,000 for the U.S.A. to $400,000,000 for India and $200,000 for Panama. As a rule 2 percent of the subscription is paid in gold and 18 percent in the member's national currency. The remaining 80 percent stands as a guarantee to cover the Bank's liabilities.

46

Most of the money the Bank lends is obtained by selling its bonds in the money markets of the world. When the Bank began operation in 1946, the great need of all countries was for dollars. The Bank had a capital nest egg of dollars from the 2 percent that each member subscribed in gold, and the United States authorized the use of its whole subscription of 635 million dollars. In 1947 the bank sold 250 million dollars worth of dollar bonds in the New York market.

Since that time, as borrowers found they could buy machinery and supplies from countries other than the United States, other currencies have come into demand. By September, 1959, the Bank had raised 2,500 million dollars to add to its own capital funds available for loans. At that time the authorized capital was increased from 10,000 million dollars to 21,000 million dollars.

The Bank can lend to a member government or one of its agencies, or to a private enterprise in a member state if the government guarantees the loan. The Bank is not in business to make money, but it must not be careless with its assets, or they would quickly melt away in a vast sea of desired but unprofitable projects all around the world.

The management of the Bank has five general principles to guide it in deciding whether to lend money in a particular case.

First, it will not use up its funds to finance any operation, however useful, if the borrower can get money from someone else on reasonable terms. This Bank is a public institution set up to increase the total of international lending, not to replace any transactions that will go on without its help.

For instance, since the first job of the Bank was to aid in the reconstruction of war-battered Europe, it started in 1947 by lending dollars to France, the Netherlands, Denmark, and Luxembourg, to be used for buying supplies mainly from North America. When the Marshall Plan came into the picture with a large supply of dollars to be spent for recovery, the Bank turned its attention to other fields of action.

The second principle is that the Bank will ordinarily lend a country only the foreign money it needs to pay for foreign supplies and services connected with a project. The Bank has to satisfy itself that the borrower is making proper efforts to raise local capital to pay for the labor and domestic materials that go into the project. For this purpose the Bank often advises on government policies to encourage local savings.

The third principle is that the borrower and guarantor must have a good prospect of paying principal and interest. Not only does the Bank have to keep its capital from being lost, but it also has to hold the confidence of investors so that they will buy its bonds.

The project must be an economically sound one in the sense that it will add more to the country's wealth than its cost. If it is a public work that draws an income, like a hydroelectric project, it will usually be able to earn enough direct income to cover its capital investment and interest. If it is a system of free roads, paid for out of tax revenues, it ought to cause an increase in the wealth of the country that would yield the necessary taxes to pay for it. The Bank wants to know that the government is efficiently administrated and that its tax system is adequate to meet the needs of a developing country.

The revenues from an enterprise, whether they are earnings or tax returns, are of course in the money of the country. The main question for the Bank is whether these revenues can be turned into dollars or whatever money is required for payments on the loan. The Bank wants to know whether the government is handling the problems of foreign exchange in such a way that the loan payments can be met along with all the ordinary costs of foreign trade.

The fourth principle is that the Bank will prefer the projects that are most useful and urgent. At best the Bank and all other sources of foreign capital cannot cover everything that growing nations would like to have. The developments include a high proportion of public or semi-public service enterprises—such as electric power plants, roads, railroads, flood control, and irrigation.

Finally, the fifth requirement is that the borrower must have the knowledge, skill, and financial position to carry the enterprise to success. Given a good basic ability to deal with the project, the borrower can get plenty of technical advice and assistance, and the Bank insists that all the necessary experts be called in. The Bank keeps up its interest in the building and operation of the enterprise during the life of the loan.

In the course of its work, the Bank sends missions to member countries, to survey particular projects or to consult on a general development program. In its general development surveys, the Bank cooperates with other agencies that may have an interest in the proposed work, especially the other specialized agencies of the UN.

One of the most notable early projects using Bank funds was the Damodar Valley Corporation in India, a development organization similar to the Tennessee Valley Authority in the United States. The original purpose of this project was to prevent the costly floods of the Damodar River. In 1945 a TVA engineer was called in, and with his advice the plans were extended to cover a full development of the river, including irrigation, navigation, and electric power. The Bank made three loans, totaling $44,500,000 mainly for electric power development in the Damodar Valley. In addition the Bank lent nearly $550,000,000 for railways, ports, aircraft, and iron and steel production and various power projects in India.

In recent years the Bank has begun to study the possibilities of atomic power for underdeveloped countries, especially those where fuel is scarce. Its first loan for this purpose was made in September, 1959, for a plant in southern Italy.

Other projects financed by the Bank have included waterpower development in Mexico, modern highways in Ethiopia, a new port in Rangoon, and pulp mills in Finland.

Another kind of work that the Bank has begun to develop is helping to find acceptable settlements for financial disputes between nations. The Bank worked out the amount that the United Arab Republic should pay to the owners of the Suez Canal, which it had seized. It also gave advice to India and Pakistan about a proposed agreement on sharing the waters of the Indus River.

The International Finance Corporation (IFC)

This agency was established in 1956 with the special purpose of encouraging the growth of private enterprises in the underdeveloped countries. It invests in such enterprises in association with private capital and management, and without requiring a government guarantee against loss. It judges projects on their merits as investments for private capital, and provides supplementary capital where it will be most useful. It does not undertake management of projects.

IFC has a capital of about 100 million dollars, subscribed by its seventy-five member governments. The projects in which it invests produce such things as lumber and rubber products, cement and prestressed concrete, cotton textiles, electrical equipment, and automobile parts.

The International Development Association (IDA)

IDA is another affiliate of the World Bank, established in 1960 to make "soft" loans for necessary public works and services that will not earn a direct income like the projects that the Bank finances, and yet will have a fair chance of repayment in course of time. Loans are made to governments or sometimes to private enterprises, with or without government guarantee. Most of the loans have been for highway construction; others have been for agricultural development, power, water supplies, and water transportation.

All the IDA credits are for a fifty-year period, with ten years' grace before repayments begin. No interest is charged, but there is a service charge of three-quarters of 1 percent per annum.

The International Monetary Fund (IMF)

The International Monetary Fund is a system of cash reserves that the member nations can draw upon to meet temporary deficits in their international trade.

The Articles of Agreement of the Fund were drawn up

by the Bretton Woods Conference in 1944, and came into
force on December 27, 1945. Nations that join the Bank
must first be members of the Fund. Each member is assigned a "quota" in the Fund and is assessed a subscription usually equal to its quota. As a rule the member pays
one-quarter of its subscription in gold, unless that would
take more than 10 percent of its official supply of gold
and dollars. The rest of the subscription is paid in the
member's own money.

When a country buys more from abroad than it can
sell abroad, it has to find some kind of foreign money to
pay the deficit. Ordinarily such payments are drawn from
the country's reserves of gold or of foreign money—generally pounds or dollars. If these reserves start to melt
away with frightening speed, the country will take some
kind of action to reduce its trade deficit.

There are some ways of dealing with a trade deficit that
are harmful to world trade, since they consist of setting
up trade barriers to keep out foreign goods. There are
other remedies that are not harmful to world trade. But
they take longer; they may not be within reach of a country with only a small reserve. The main purpose of the
Fund is to be a supplementary reserve that in favorable
cases will make possible a sound adjustment of the member's international trade position.

The Directors of the Fund have discretionary powers to
restrict or expand the amount of help they will give to a
member, according to whether they think the member is
taking the correct actions to balance its trade. The Fund
cannot encourage a member simply to lean on the Fund
when it has a deficit, without doing anything to cure the
deficit. Such actions would fritter away the Fund's hard
currency without lasting benefit to the members. The
Directors therefore consult regularly with the member
governments about their financial policies and advise them
about possible improvements.

The Fund is particularly interested in bringing about
what is known as "convertibility." The British pound
sterling, for instance, is convertible if a dealer coming into
the money market with a thousand pounds can freely
change them for dollars, francs, or any other kind of

money he might want. Another ideal is the stabilization of exchange value. The pound is stable if it will always bring the same number of dollars or ounces of gold.

If a country has been having trouble keeping its reserves, it may resort to exchange restrictions of some kind, which limit the amount of that country's money that anyone can turn into gold or dollars. If the country decides to make its money convertible, it removes these restrictions. But it looks with apprehension at what may happen next.

The chief danger, when money is made convertible, is that it may be exposed in time of stress to a heavy demand for converting the local money into foreign currencies. This creates a "run on the bank" that might be disastrous. If such a run develops, the "bank may have to close." That is, the government puts back the exchange restrictions, and is left in a weaker position than before.

Why, then, should a country want to take the risks of removing exchange restrictions? The removal is an exercise of financial strength to take advantage of the profits of free trade. The country can then shop around freely to buy its imports wherever it can get the best bargains. It will also have to sell abroad in unprotected competition with its rivals. This necessity may scare some of its businessmen, but if they can stand it they will become more productive and safer against inflation of their costs.

If all the principal countries can make their money convertible, world trade will be increased and will be more efficient. Goods will be bought and sold in the most profitable markets. The Fund devotes much of its attention to advising nations on how to become financially strong enough to take the risks of convertibility with good prospects of success.

There are two kinds of devices that countries can use for balancing their trade when they are failing to sell enough abroad to balance what they buy. One kind of treatment is designed to make people in the country buy less from abroad; the other kind is designed to get foreigners to buy more of what the country has to sell. The first kind includes tariffs, which raise the prices of foreign goods in the country. It also includes restrictions on imports or in the use of money, which directly cut down the buying of foreign goods. The international trade organizations aim to persuade countries to avoid these devices as far as possible, since they stifle trade.

The second kind of treatment for balancing trade is made up of devices for selling more goods to foreigners. One way is to "devalue" the currency, or reduce its value in ounces of gold. Then a foreigner with gold or its equivalent can buy more of the devalued money than before. This is the same as offering a special discount to foreign buyers, for the internal prices paid by citizens do not change much, if any, when the money is devalued in gold. The United States devalued the dollar in 1933 to promote exports; and the countries of Western Europe devalued their currencies in 1949.

The members of the Fund have agreed not to devalue their money more than 10 percent without getting the advice of the Fund. Frequent changes in the value of money are disturbing to trade because they make dealers fear to sign contracts for future payments.

The device that is most approved for stimulating exports is to keep prices down—in other words, to avoid inflation. If there is not too much money in circulation in the country, compared with the goods and services for sale, prices will hold down, and foreign buyers will be attracted. On the other hand, if there is too little money, there will be deflation, and prices will fall so far as to cause unemployment. The government's problem is to adopt policies that will lead to the correct balance between inflation and deflation, and the correct balance between encouraging exports and maintaining full employment.

If the government knows how to adopt the right policies, and if the voters will stand the short-term discomforts that go with such policies, a country may be able to balance its affairs internally and externally at the same time. Since this condition leads in the long run to the highest combination of prosperity and real income, it is worth some sacrifices if it can be attained. The Monetary Fund advises the members on how to attain the right balance.

The exact measures that are needed to put a country in sound condition vary with circumstances, but in the main they consist of actions that governments can take if they are allowed to do so by the voters.

To prevent inflation there are two principal financial devices. One is to raise taxes and cut public spending until the correct state of budget balance is reached. The other is to raise the government "discount rate," which will cause higher interest rates generally and discourage borrowing. The discount rate is the rate of interest that the commercial banks have to pay if they borrow from the central bank, or, in the United States, from the Federal Reserve banks.

The general principle of budget balance, now well understood by financial experts, is that in depression the government should run a deficit so as to give the people more money to spend. Then if a boom comes on, the government should reverse and run a surplus, so the people will have less money to spend. If the price level is satisfactory as it is, then the budget should have only enough deficit to create the money each year that is needed to carry on the growing volume of business. No one can hit the ideal level exactly, but governments can come close enough to do fairly well in stabilizing prices.

The reason for raising the discount rate in a threatened inflation is that too many people are borrowing money from the banks to use for investment or spending. If interest rates go up they may put a damper on this borrowing. The effect is not as powerful as the effect of budgetary changes. Many countries leave their official discount rates unchanged for years at a stretch.

Aside from these two financial devices, the principal way to avoid inflation is by speeding the advance of technology. Increased efficiency of production reduces costs and allows prices to come down while real wages go up. This is the most valuable adjustment, but it takes a long time. It serves as underpinning for the sound financial policies that are able to take effect more rapidly.

In the underdeveloped countries, the inflation danger is likely to arise in connection with economic development. New factories can be built with the people's savings, or with foreign money invested in the country, with comparatively little danger. But if the program is pushed too fast it may be financed by government borrowing from the banks, which is in effect the same as printing the money. Too much of this may poison the new development with inflated prices that discourage real savings and chill the whole program. The techniques for holding to a sound development policy call for expert advice which can be obtained from the Bank and the Fund.

How does the Monetary Fund do its work? First of all, it consults with countries that are protecting their trade balance by artificial trade barriers, advising what policies to adopt for improving their fundamental strength. Then it stands ready to help out as the member countries take one step after another toward freer trade.

Each time a country loosens up on the bandage that is restricting its trade, it may start to bleed a little from its gold and dollar reserve. If the loss is soon stanched, the new adjustment is a success. The circulation is improved and the country is stronger. During this process, the country may supplement its own reserve by purchasing the currency it needs from the Fund, paying in its own currency. It may need dollars or pounds or some other money to take care of a temporary deficit while trade is getting adjusted to the new rules.

When a country is past the adjustment period, and has built its reserve to a new safe level, it can restore its position in the Fund by buying back its own currency for dollars, or other freely convertible currencies, or for gold. By April 30, 1964, members of the Fund had repurchased over 5,000 million dollars worth of their currencies.

The amounts that members can get from the Fund are limited in various ways. They have almost free rights to draw currency to the amount of their gold deposit, and a limited right to sums in excess of that, with an overall limit generally equal to their quota. The Directors may allow a country a standby account that it can draw upon in case of need. They can stretch these limits for specially useful adjustments that the Fund wants to encourage. The Fund provides money only for adjustments that it is convinced can be carried through in three to five years. It is not in the business of making long-term investments.

For each accommodation the member pays the Fund a service charge of 0.5 percent. If the amount purchased is larger than the member's gold subscription, he pays an additional charge which starts three months after the transaction at 2 percent a year and increases with time and with the size of the purchase in relation to the member's quota. These stepped-up charges are intended to put pressure on the member to set his house in order and buy back his currency. The money received is used to defray the Fund's expenses, though that is not its chief purpose.

In the first years after 1945, the Monetary Fund made little progress in the field of exchange restrictions. Nor did it permit many drawings on its resources. The troubles of the member nations were so deep-seated that no temporary help could cure them. For the time, they had to protect themselves with trade barriers until they could build up their production. But as the war damage has been repaired and business has improved, the Fund has had more and more opportunities to promote the free exchange of money that is the lifeblood of healthy world trade.

By April, 1964, the Fund had 102 members, and had sold various currencies equivalent to a total of nearly 7,600 million dollars.

During 1959 and 1960 most of the members voluntarily increased their subscriptions by 50 to 100 percent. The total assets of the Fund, which in January, 1959, amounted to 9,200 million dollars, were increased through new subscriptions to nearly 16,000 million dollars by 1964.

On the whole the members have continued to keep their policies in line with the Fund's objectives, and each year has brought some degree of progress toward currency convertibility. They have made increasing use of the opportunities for technical cooperation, and have become well accustomed to referring important questions of foreign exchange policy to the Fund for advice.

In 1964 the world trade situation was increasingly favorable. Many of the less-developed countries were enjoying an improvement in the prices of the raw materials they had for sale. They therefore had more foreign money to use in buying machinery and other goods needed for development. The United States, which had been suffering an adverse balance of payments for several years, was doing better, since its prices were not rising as rapidly as those of its chief competitors in Europe.

But the IMF was concerned about the future supply of

international money for handling a rapidly growing volume of world trade. The supply of new gold coming into the market was not enough to maintain the proportion of gold to the volume of payments, and more and more reliance would have to be placed on faith in the stable value of the dollar and other trading units. In the IMF the feeling was growing that the best way to protect "liquidity" or free-flowing international money would be to increase the IMF quotas and make more habitual use of the IMF in even small fluctuations of trade balances. There was also some talk of increasing the weight of the IMF by allowing it to accept deposits like a bank, and also to make investments.

General Agreement on Tariffs and Trade (GATT)

In 1945 the Economic and Social Council decided to call a Conference on Trade and Employment, with the hope of reducing tariffs and other trade barriers.

This led to the establishment of the General Agreement on Tariffs and Trade, known as GATT. The United States and all the other principal trading nations joined in the GATT conferences.

In these conferences, each member nation comes in with a list of other people's tariffs that it hopes to get reduced, and a list of its own tariffs that it might reduce in the course of bargaining. The rule is that if any two countries agree to reduce certain tariffs for each other's benefit, they must give everyone else the same reduction. An exception is made for the underdeveloped nations, many of which have joined GATT in recent years. A developing nation needs to be granted special favors in the way of low tariffs on the manufactures that it wants to sell to the industrialized countries. It also needs to set relatively high tariffs on its imports from the advanced nations, while granting easy entrance to imports from other developing countries. Free trade is desirable and practical only between economic equals.

The conferences also take up other kinds of trade barriers, and consider complaints about members that violate their agreements.

The effect of GATT has been a notable reduction in obstacles to trade. Along with the Bank's assistance to the international flow of capital, and the Fund's help in the exchange of money, the general situation of world production and trade since the Bretton Woods Conference has shown an encouraging rate of improvement.

Conference on Trade and Development of 1964

The fact that traditional trade practices place almost insurmountable obstacles in the path of the developing nations has been widely discussed in the UN, and in 1964 interest in this problem led to a world conference at Geneva attended by 119 nations. The conference met from March 23 to June 16.

One problem is the imbalance between the prices of raw materials sold by the developing countries and those of the manufactured goods they need to buy. Both sets of prices are controlled by market forces in the industrialized nations. A closely allied problem results from the advanced nations' habit of levying tariffs against manufactured goods that the poorer countries might produce and sell in world trade. Along with unfair shipping charges and other practices the overall effect is to make the rich richer and the poor poorer. Yet all the nations say they want to help the developing countries, and in the main they mean it.

At the conference the developing nations naturally were in the majority, but economic power rested with the advanced countries so there was no point in merely voting. Much time, therefore, was profitably spent in discussion and negotiation. The outcome was a series of resolutions expressing the intention of negotiating further, with a view to improving the balance of trade and giving the developing countries a chance to make progress.

The conference recommended that the UN Assembly set up a permanent organization to watch over the complicated world trade network and to keep the pressure of world opinion on the side of policies favorable to development. If these proposals are successful they will mark an important advance toward world prosperity.

—4—

TECHNICAL SERVICES

The modern world depends on many kinds of technical service to make possible the most efficient production and distribution. Some of the necessary services have to be international. Several UN specialized agencies are devoted to providing these international technical services. It is noteworthy that these technical organizations, which deal only with experts and are generally unknown to the ordinary man in the street, began to appear long before the grass-roots services such as WHO and FAO. Probably the main reason for this difference in timing is that the techniques for directly attacking disease and poverty developed later than those for services such as telegraph and mail. The progress of international action from legalistic and technical abstractions to the provision of human everyday services is one of the main reasons for the increasing vitality of the idea of international cooperation.

International Telecommunication Union (ITU)

ITU is the oldest of the specialized agencies, having been founded as the International Telegraph Union in 1865 in Paris. In 1932 the radio agreements were added. A revised governing Convention went into effect at the beginning of 1954. The central office of ITU is in Geneva.

The principal work of ITU is to persuade the nations to agree to a practical allocation of radio frequency bands. It also tries to establish the lowest practicable rate schedules for radio, telegraph, and telephone services. ITU committees study and report on engineering problems, from radio ground-wave propagation to the design of telegraph apparatus and the protection of telephone lines from corrosion. ITU publishes technical literature and collects and reports on technical papers published by others.

The Administrative Radio Conference of the ITU which met in Geneva in 1959 had two main problems: the establishment of an international frequency list and the preparation of a plan for high-frequency broadcasting. The radio spectrum has to be allocated to many different types of service, such as maritime, aeronautical, and spaceship communications, weather reporting, broadcasting including TV, amateur radio, and various kinds of scientific work including astronomy.

ITU takes part in the Expanded Program of Technical Assistance, sending experts to advise countries that are developing their communications, and granting fellowships for specialists to study abroad. In Ethiopia, for instance, by 1960 more than five hundred telecommunications employees had been trained in fourteen different subjects in an ITU institute. In April, 1963, ITU launched a plan for an African communications network, known as the Dakar Plan.

Universal Postal Union (UPU)

The Universal Postal Union was established in 1875. In that year the Universal Postal Convention, proposed by the Postal Congress of Berne, Switzerland, in 1874, came into force. Meetings of the Postal Congress are held every five years to examine the rules of UPU and keep them up to date. From the beginning the members agreed that for a reasonable charge every member would have the right to send its mail over any other member's transport services, and that mail coming in from abroad would be delivered without extra charge. The members are also pledged to handle foreign mail by the best means of transport used for domestic mail.

The international postal services include not only letter mail but also parcel post, insured mail, money orders and traveler's checks, collection of bills, and subscriptions to newspapers and magazines.

UPU has set up a Consultative Commission on Postal Studies, to collect information on new technical methods such as mechanized sorting, stamp-selling machines, the most efficient organization of post offices, and the use of special rates for jet-plane service. UPU advises the UN in technical assistance on postal questions, and makes arrangements between different countries for "direct technical assistance" by exchange of specialists and information.

A nation may join UPU if two thirds of the members agree. Headquarters are in Berne.

International Civil Aviation Organization (ICAO)

In 1919 an International Commission for Air Navigation was formed in Paris to set up technical standards, and in 1928 the Pan American Convention on Commercial Aviation was drawn up at Havana. These earlier agreements were superseded by the Convention on International Civil Aviation, drafted at a conference in Chicago in 1944. ICAO came into effect on April 4, 1947, on the proposal being ratified by twenty-six states.

The chief purposes of ICAO are to promote safety and technical progress in aviation, and to see to it that the member states are fairly treated in the operation of airlines. Since 1945, ICAO has helped its 105 member nations to coordinate the services required for international air transport—such as weather reports, traffic control, radio aids, and communications. Ocean weather stations also aid surface craft and provide search and rescue services. ICAO arranges special aids for air navigation over sparsely settled areas or regions of uncertain sovereignty.

ICAO cooperates in UN technical assistance, especially in helping the less-developed countries to set up ground services for civil aviation, and in pilot training, instruction in aircraft maintenance, and the organizing of airlines and government civil aviation departments.

To improve air safety, ICAO has introduced international standards and recommended practices which are now in effect in all member countries. These codes cover such questions as the licensing of pilots; the right of way in the air; traffic controls; airworthiness; and the simplification of customs, immigration, and inspection regulations at airports. ICAO deals with the organization to be provided by each member to rescue the victims of aircraft accidents, and the system of inquiry into the causes of accidents. As an example of the overall improvement in air safety, ICAO reports that while the deaths per hundred million passenger-miles in 1945 had been 4.9, in 1963 they were only 0.76, one sixth as many.

ICAO has drafted international air law agreements on various questions, such as recognition of property rights in aircraft, compensation for damage caused by foreign aircraft falling in a country, and crimes committed on board aircraft. ICAO is also making a special study of the problems of supersonic aircraft.

World Meteorological Organization (WMO)

Weather forecasting is important in a great number of activities, from agriculture and aviation to shipping and the management of recreational enterprises. Since forecasting is based on wide-ranging information on existing conditions in distant places, it depends on close international cooperation, which is the main reason for the existence of WMO.

Forecasting is not the only aspect of weather that is important. Another major field of knowledge is climate, a sort of long-range analysis that tells the engineer what rainfall and streamflow to provide for in building dams and bridges, and that tells the agricultural expert about hot, cold, wet, and dry conditions that may invite or prohibit the use of certain crops. WMO acts as an international authority prepared to help a member country in the study of its climate.

In its main job of improving the forecasting of sunshine, wind, and rain, WMO helps the member nations to develop a worldwide network of weather observation stations. At regular intervals every day, trained observers all over the world take the standard observations of temperature, wind, rainfall, and other features of the weather, all at exactly the same moment, be it day or night locally. Some stations are on the surface of the land, some in ships at sea, some in airplanes, and some in weather satellites swinging around the earth and sending television pictures of the clouds as seen from above.

Altogether, in 1964, there were some 8,000 land stations, 4,000 on ships at sea, and 3,000 on aircraft in flight; and the number increases each year.

The observations are fed into a global communications network that takes them to centers where electronic computers rapidly digest the information. The results are then flashed to the nations where they are needed. The system, which WMO has named the World Weather Watch, is being constantly extended and improved as new methods are invented and new networks established.

WMO is studying with ICAO the relation of weather to the use of supersonic airplanes, in preparation for the expected use of supersonic transport planes in the near future. It is also studying and reporting on radioactivity of the atmosphere, at the request of the UN General Assembly.

WMO offers technical assistance to countries that ask for help in expanding their weather departments, and in the training of people to work in them. For example, in 1959 it undertook to help the Government of Chile in the measurement of rainfall and streamflow, the information to be used as a basis for the development of waterpower. By 1963 the project had set up some 114 stations to measure rainfall, 63 to measure streamflow, and 40 to study climate, with people trained to establish and manage such stations. In one river valley, where a power project was already in an advanced stage of planning, the new observations showed that total potential waterpower of the basin was three times as much as what had been estimated on the basis of the previous scanty information.

Control of Narcotics Trade

International traffic in habit-forming drugs is controlled by the producing and importing nations under terms of a series of treaties made between 1912 and 1948. Legal shipments to each receiving country are based on technical estimates of that country's needs for medical and scientific purposes, and the producing countries are under obligation not to export more than the required quotas.

The enforcement of these treaties is supervised by three United Nations organs, the Commission on Narcotic Drugs —successor to a similar committee of the League of Nations—and two specialized agencies, the Permanent Central Opium Board and the Drug Supervisory Body. These agencies handle the estimates and trade statistics that govern the quantities of various drugs that can be legally shipped.

Not all countries are parties to the drug treaties, but since a legal shipment of any dangerous drug must have both an export permit and an import permit, it is hard for any country to avoid the system. There is, of course, some smuggling, and sometimes a country evades the rules. But world public opinion is so strongly set against illicit drug trading that all governments are sensitive to the effects on their international standing if they are accused of cheating in their relations with the UN system of supervision.

Intergovernmental Maritime Consultative Organization (IMCO)

IMCO was established in January, 1959, to promote the highest standards of navigation and safety at sea. Among its first activities was the proposal of two international agreements, one on safety and one on prevention of pollution of the sea by oil. Other interests of the organization are the promotion of uniformity in measurement of ship tonnage, and the simplification of the voluminous paper work required for ships entering or leaving port. Headquarters of IMCO are in London.

A conference was held in the summer of 1960 to revise the earlier agreements on safety rules and related matters. A new feature was a set of provisions and recommendations in regard to nuclear ships, which are strongly opposed by many influential shipping interests because of the dangers of contamination in case of collision or shipwreck. There were new recommendations on ship construction and on the establishment of a set of rules for the transport of dangerous goods. IMCO cooperates with ICAO, ITU, and WMO in devising methods for rescue of the victims of ship or airplane wrecks at sea. IMCO has also assumed responsibility for revising the international code of signals.

The Expanded Program

Most of these technical services are carried out by the UN family of agencies with help and coordinating advice from two general programs, the Expanded Program of Technical Assistance and the Special Fund. These programs are supported by voluntary contributions of the member nations, the main purpose being to assure a full range of services that will aid the developing countries.

The Expanded Program was adopted as a result of the worldwide interest aroused in 1949 when President Harry S. Truman of the United States, in his inaugural address, proposed a "bold new program" of economic progress for the less-developed countries of the world. The UN Charter had recognized that there was a growing demand for economic development, and with this new encouragement the UN was able to add new emphasis to its technical assistance activities. A special fund was set up in 1950 to which 54 nations pledged $20,000,000 for the first eighteen months of the new program. By the middle of 1964 the number of contributing governments had risen to 108, and the total of contributions was about $51,-000,000 for the one year.

The UN and nine related agencies share in the funds available each year to operate the Expanded Program. A Technical Assistance Board, made up of representatives of the ten participants and headed by an Executive Chairman, coordinates the Program. Within the UN itself, the Bureau of Technical Assistance Operations takes responsibility for projects that do not come within the field of any one Agency—such as general development plans, a national income census, town planning, industrial development programs, and land and inland water transport.

In its first fourteen years the Expanded Program of Technical Assistance sent out over 12,500 experts who came from ninety countries or territories. It gave 26,000 fellowships for students from less-developed countries to study abroad, and made modest grants of equipment and supplies. Cutting across those classifications are numerous training institutions, seminars, and group study tours. With the aid of the International Atomic Energy Agency and the specialized agencies, the program has been able to respond to requests for help in nearly all technical fields of work.

The Decade of Development

In 1961 the General Assembly unanimously adopted a resolution declaring the 1960's to be the UN Development Decade. This action was brought about by a realization that in the 1950's, despite massive economic aid from all sources, and despite the efforts of the governments themselves, the gap between the poorer and the richer nations had widened.

The general target of the Development Decade is to bring all the less-developed countries up to a growth rate of not less than 5 percent per year. Some of the most advanced countries grow much more slowly than that. At the end of the 1950's, for instance, the United States was growing about 3 percent and the United Kingdom about 2.5 percent per year. But Mexico's growth rate was 5.7 percent, Turkey's 6.5, the Philippines' 5.7, and Taiwan's 6.1, indicating that less-developed countries can grow rapidly if conditions are favorable.

The Economic and Social Council has been particularly concerned with the activities of the UN family in connection with the Development Decade. In 1963 it listed four main areas needing special attention. One was the trade obstacles that face the developing countries—the falling markets for most of the raw materials they have to sell, and the tariff barriers against their manufactures if they try to work up their raw materials for export. Other areas were the need for assistance in the building of new industries, the problems of applying science and technology in less-developed areas, and the lack of schools and training systems.

One of the first events organized by the UN to give a start to the Development Decade was an International Conference on the Application of Science and Technology for the Benefit of the Less-Developed Countries. At the same time, FAO dramatized the most urgent goal of the Decade by launching its five-year Freedom-from-Hunger Campaign, and by calling, in June, 1963, a World Food Congress. The Congress, in turn, led to the initiation of the joint UN-FAO World Food Program.

Artesian Basins Under Deserts

One example of new knowledge brought out by the Science and Technology Conference was the fact that there is an artesian water basin in North Africa that extends under Morocco, Tunisia, Algeria, and Central Africa. Another one underlies parts of Libya and Egypt, bringing water from the Sudan and Ethiopia, and still other great basins exist under Arabia and under the Gobi Desert in central Asia.

An artesian basin can be drained if more water is drawn out of the wells than is replaced by rainfall in the high country from where the water comes. After all, these are only vast underground piping systems transporting water from place to place, often from a rainy country to a desert one. If one desert country draws more than its fair share of the supply, others will hasten to seize their share, and more, and in a generation or so the costly development based on the welcome water supplies will dry up the underground water, and fall into poverty and desolation.

To measure the supply, and to persuade the countries that draw from the same basin to agree on their shares and honestly limit their drafts on the underground water to an agreed allocation, are jobs for the United Nations.

Power for Development

One of the most important features of modern progress in the underdeveloped regions of the world is the supplying of electricity to small villages and farms. The UN is deeply interested in ways to produce small quantities of power at a cost that poor people can afford, in localities where cheap waterpower, oil, or coal are not to be had.

The exciting prospect of using atomic power for such purposes died down as soon as the practical difficulties began to be well recognized. Atomic power is not yet cheap; it costs more than the usual kinds of power. It is not adapted to small plants; a big atomic plant has to be located near a big market, such as a large city or industrial area, or a grid in a highly developed country.

Ordinary electricity can be brought to farms and villages by a high-voltage distribution system, but only in a well-developed country where the farmers have a higher income than they have in most of the world. For the majority of farmers and villagers throughout the world the only hope of seeing any practical kind of electrical power is in the use of small-scale local sources.

The UN Conference on New Sources of Energy, held in Rome in August, 1961, brought together nearly 450 technical experts to discuss the possibilities of power from wind, sun, and underground heat, all of which are widely distributed and usable on a fairly small scale. These "new" sources of energy are new to the modern world because scientists and inventors have found new ways of using them that greatly reduce their cost.

Windmills, for instance, can now be had in all sizes and all degrees of modernization, from the household type to a great 900-kilowatt plant for connection to a city system. Of most interest for underdeveloped areas are the small mills for a single farm or a village. The first use of a small power plant is usually for pumping water, but there is a growing tendency to produce electricity instead of merely connecting the windmill directly to the pump. The electricity costs far more per kilowatt-hour than the current from a large plant in a city, but the value of a few hundred watts, instead of none at all, is out of all proportion to the unit costs. In a village, where diesel oil may be expensive, a small diesel generating plant, with a windmill to save oil whenever the wind blows, will often be the most valuable start toward rapid modernization.

The energy of the sun has long been used directly for drying fish and farm products and for evaporating sea-water. The Conference received 118 papers on the uses of solar energy for producing electricity and for other purposes. Most of the poorest agricultural populations live in the hotter zones of the earth, where the sunshine is most plentiful except in the rainy season. The technology of collecting and utilizing the sun's energy has developed rapidly in recent years, partly because of its use in the operation of spaceships. Many of the new inventions can be used on a small scale, and some of them are cheap enough to be employed by country folk who have only small money-incomes.

The earth's heat is used on a large scale to produce electricity in Italy, and for heating buildings in Iceland. Other "geothermal" plants are found in many scattered parts of the world. The earth's heat can be drawn upon in places where an underground supply of water is in contact with hot rocks under a tight layer of rock that holds in the steam until it is tapped by a bored well. Such conditions are not uncommon throughout the world, and the technical methods of prospecting for new fields have been well developed. A natural-steam plant may be a more costly enterprise than a village diesel-and-wind combination, but if the village and its industries can make profitable use of the power, it has the advantage of continuous service with no fuel cost.

The many encouraging lines of progress in small-scale power plants can be expected to transform the lives of millions of farm and village people within the next generation or two.

The Population Explosion

It is obvious that the goals of the United Nations Development Decade will be seriously undercut by the increase of population. In the 17th General Assembly this fact was recognized in an important resolution on "Population Growth and Economic Development," passed by a vote of 69 to 0 with 27 abstaining.

The resolution directed the Secretary-General to inquire of the member states about their population problems in relation to development. It also directed the various UN agencies to intensify their studies of these questions and to help the less-developed nations in obtaining information on the subject. Finally, the World Population Conference scheduled for 1965 was requested to emphasize the relationship between population and economic development.

In the debate on this resolution, four main viewpoints

were disclosed. The resolution was favored by such widely scattered countries as Sweden, Ceylon, Uganda, Japan, and India. On the other side were Ireland, Argentina, and other Latin-American countries that questioned the existence of any such problem and denied the right of the UN to mention the subject. A more moderate view, held by France and some French-African and Latin-American states, was that UN action should be postponed until more study had been done. Finally, the communist position was that no population problems could exist under communism. In the end, no one voted against the resolution, though some members did not vote.

This debate is a notable example of the value of the United Nations as a forum for discussion. The population explosion is, next to the atom, the most serious danger now facing the human race; yet no nation acting alone can hint to another nation, especially a less prosperous one, that its people are too numerous and are not wanted on earth. Only the UN, acting on the motion of a group of small nations, many of them underdeveloped, could tackle so delicate a problem.

Another important outcome of this debate was a change in the position of the Soviet Union. The communist theory that population cannot be too numerous for a nation's natural resources was given a cold reception by the Assembly. In the vote, the Soviet bloc abstained; there are signs of a willingness to cooperate in a realistic approach to the population problem. Although there is still much difference of opinion among the world's cultures and religions as to which methods of population control are morally permissible, there is no important religious or ideological doctrine that denies the need for control.

In December, 1963, an Asian Population Conference was held in New Delhi under the auspices of the Economic Commission for Asia and the Far East and the UN Bureau of Social Affairs. Prime Minister Nehru pointed out that population growth in India was alarming and that population was racing with economic progress.

U Nyun, Executive Secretary of the Economic Commission for Asia and the Far East, told the conference that the population explosion in Asia threatened to wash out the gains from economic development. He declared that each government would have to decide its own population policy, but that all governments should have available the latest knowledge on methods of birth control.

The Special Fund

The UN Special Fund was inaugurated January 1, 1959, with a budget of $26,000,000 raised by voluntary contributions of governments. It is designed to fill in the gaps between programs of the other agencies in the less-developed countries, particularly the gaps in knowledge of what resources are available, and in the number of trained technicians to undertake their development. The Fund makes arrangements with one of the UN agencies to do the needed work.

As a matter of policy the Fund concentrates on a limited number of fairly large projects. It is particularly interested in providing resource surveys and research to bring out the best uses of special raw materials or other natural resources that may be found in a country. It also helps in establishing technical courses to train the many kinds of engineers, teachers, transport and communications workers, health workers, public administrators, and other skilled people who make up the working body of a modern civilized community. It promotes demonstrations of new methods, including pilot projects. The basic purpose of these programs is to open the way for a more rapid increase of public works and private investment, so that national incomes and standards of living can be raised as quickly as possible.

The Fund does not supply investment capital, which has to come from other sources. Its work is to trigger investment by these other sources. In mid-1964 the Fund was assisting 421 major projects in 130 low-income countries and territories, at a total cost of nearly 1,000 million dollars. The Fund pays about 40 percent of the cost of these projects; the other 60 percent is paid by the developing countries themselves.

These activities are highly profitable to the developing countries. The "seed effect" can be illustrated by the fact that ten resource surveys costing some 10 million dollars immediately led to investment of more than 755 million dollars of domestic and foreign capital.

By 1964 the Fund was helping 170 training institutions in developing countries. These institutions had already upgraded the skills of more than 50,000 urgently needed engineers and technicians, managers and supervisors, industrial instructors, high-school teachers, planners, and skilled transport and communications workers. More than a third of these are teachers who serve to multiply the effect. The Fund is also helping 84 applied research institutes, which study ways to promote better use of local materials, invention of new products, and improvement of manufacturing techniques.

The Special Fund, which has grown to be the largest UN agency for technical cooperation, works closely with the Expanded Program, and uses the same field offices as that program.

Economic Commission for Europe (ECE)

ECE, set up by the Economic and Social Council in 1946, is one of four UN regional economic commissions. The others cover Latin America, Asia and the Far East, and Africa.

At first the main purpose of the regional organizations was to handle the specifically regional problems that arise in the economic relations among neighboring countries. In recent years these commissions have been developed more and more as centers for the work of the UN and its specialized agencies. WHO, especially, has come to operate mainly through regional organizations, and other UN agencies are moving in the same direction. In 1961 the General Assembly expressed the hope that the Special Fund would aid the establishment of Economic Development Institutes at the seats of the four regional commissions.

In 1946 the most urgent problem in Europe was to revive production and trade, so that people could eat and could repair the devastation of war. The United Nations Economic and Social Council, which was established in that year, examined the situation in Europe and suggested a regional organization to coordinate reconstruction work.

The Assembly in December, 1946, directed the Council to establish an Economic Commission for Europe.

All the European states that belong to the UN are members of ECE, together with the United States. European states that do not belong to the UN are allowed to attend ECE meetings and to take part in committee work. The Commission meets once a year; most of the ECE work is done by special committees. The staff is part of the UN Secretariat.

One of the most valuable features of ECE is that of all the regional organizations in Europe it alone, being directly under UN administration, has members from both Eastern and Western Europe.

ECE committees carry on a vast amount of technical work that is necessary for the smooth running of trade and industry in Europe. They arrange for the return of railroad cars, allocate scarce coal supplies, and promote standardization of spare parts. The ECE Committee on Agriculture studies and reports on such matters as farming methods for small farmers, tenancy regulations, and cooperative credit. The Committee on Electric Power makes technical studies and helps to untangle the legal problems of hydroelectric projects on boundary rivers. Other committees deal with the engineering industry, housing, steel, timber, inland transport, and the development of trade.

The staff of ECE issues an annual *Economic Survey of Europe* and a quarterly *Economic Bulletin for Europe,* which are authoritative guides for many kinds of economic planning by European governments.

ECE also takes a direct interest in the development of the less advanced economic systems in other regions, and in planning ways in which the European countries can help them. In particular, it has called the attention of its member governments to the need for more generous trade policies in the admission of products from the poorer countries that desperately need to earn foreign money to pay for development. The developing countries do not need only to export raw materials, their chief source of export earnings in the past, but they need also to export manufactured goods and semi-processed materials, many of which come into competition with European manufactures and often meet with trade barriers such as tariffs or quotas.

The advanced countries, in their efforts to help in development, need to underpin these efforts by finding ways to remove such trade barriers, probably through paying compensation to certain domestic industries that will be hurt by increased imports.

ECE offers help to other regional commissions in various ways. It has sent some of its staff, for instance, to help in the organization of the young Economic Commission for Africa. It has sent out reports on technical improvements in steel-making, particularly in open hearth and electric furnaces, which have the vital advantage of producing steel economically in a relatively small plant. Another technical development studied by ECE is the transportation by sea of liquefied natural gas in tankers; this product has a ready market in European countries and produces a welcome income for less-developed areas.

Economic Commission for Asia and the Far East (ECAFE)

ECAFE is one of four regional commissions attached to the UN Economic and Social Council. This is the first organization in history that has brought together most of the nations of the Orient to discuss their problems and plans. Its main task is to help in developing the production and trade of the area extending from Pakistan to Japan, including the islands of the Western Pacific. ECAFE headquarters are in Bangkok, Thailand.

In connection with industrial development, for instance, ECAFE has studied the general conditions for effective foreign aid programs, has recommended the development of national income and resource budgets, and has suggested principles for planning how to bring in new industries without upsetting regular employment and the standard of living.

ECAFE has made surveys and supplied information about developments in the steel industry, electric power, mineral resources, small-scale industries, housing, and building materials. It has given special attention to the problems of financing economic growth, the promotion of trade, and the design of flood control and water resource conservation. It has cooperated with FAO in a study of the economics of agriculture and in promoting land reform. ECAFE helps in the organization of training centers and study tours. In 1949 it organized a conference in Singapore on inland transport, out of which grew the Inland Water Transport Tour, mentioned in Chapter 1.

ECAFE's Bureau of Flood Control and Water Resources Development has organized a project for surveying the resources of the Mekong River, one of the greatest rivers of the world, which runs out of the mountains of Tibet through the countries of Laos, Thailand, Cambodia, and South Vietnam.

The Mekong development, if it is not interrupted by hostile invasions from the north, will be somewhat like the Tennessee Valley development in the United States, but much larger. It will bring to prosperity some of the world's most underdeveloped areas, and it will strengthen peace in Southeast Asia by establishing close cooperation among four neighboring nations. Many outside countries are cooperating in this project. Australia is contributing geological surveys; Canada is making aerial maps. France sends hydrological equipment, and surveys soils and fisheries. India provides rain gauges, and Iran, petroleum products. New Zealand and the United Kingdom have built boats for the project; Japan is making reconnaissance surveys; and the United States has set up a network of streamflow and weather recording stations. Pakistan contributes experts on irrigation and flood control; Israel has offered a thousand tons of cement. The UN specialized agencies and the Special Fund are also taking part in the enterprise.

Economic Commission for Latin America (ECLA)

This commission is composed of representatives of all the nations that have territories in the Western Hemisphere —the American countries and France, Holland, and the United Kingdom. ECLA has headquarters at Santiago, Chile, and a branch office in Mexico City. It deals with the planning and management of economic development.

The Commission has discussed how to make more capital available in the Latin-American countries, both by attracting more foreign investment and by encouraging local savings. It has recommended that the Latin-American nations expand trade among themselves, especially by improving transport facilities. It has made studies of agricultural credit, forestry, mineral resources, and trade problems, including balance of payments. The Commission studies how to expand the trade of Latin America with Europe and the United States. It has asked member governments to consider encouraging the immigration of European workers as well as migration within Latin America.

Other subjects that the Commission has worked upon include rural health, tourism, supplies for educational institutions, and arrangements for cooperation with the Inter-American Economic and Social Council. ECLA studies of trade in Latin America have stimulated the Central American nations to undertake the organization of a common market free of trade barriers among themselves, and similar studies are under way for the rest of Latin America.

Economic Commission for Africa (ECA)

ECA was established in 1958 to aid in coordinating the economic and social development of the African nations and territories. In addition to the rapid emergence of independent states in Africa, economic and social progress there has also been impressive since World War II.

Governments in Africa are taking an active interest in promoting the growth of agriculture and industry. Countries that have depended mainly on subsistence farming, together with organized production of a few export crops or minerals, are turning to modern diversified economic activity, with all its problems as well as its advantages. These developments are the particular field of interest for ECA.

In 1963 the Commission issued a report on the possibilities of establishing a Common Market, beginning with agricultural products that are now generally traded among the African nations without tariffs, and proceeding with imported goods not yet produced in any African state.

Later the free trade could be extended to goods produced in the area.

In October, 1963, the Commission held a conference at Addis Ababa on African electric power development. There were sixty experts from twenty-one African countries and fifty-three from countries outside Africa. The conference discussed the opportunities for early development and interchange of power, and proposals for the training of African technicians in electrical work.

All these technical service agencies and commissions deal with the organization of the modern economic system. Many of them are unknown to the ordinary man in the street or the man on the farm, but what they are doing makes the difference between primitive ways of living and the full use of science and invention.

The technical services are more closely related to the behavior of governments than they are to the everyday thinking of the people. These commissions and conferences bring together the experts from all over the world to discuss hard scientific facts. They decide what needs to be done in order that industry and trade can be carried on efficiently. Then they report to their home governments, putting them under pressure to cooperate in a great network of practical relationships.

The network of cooperative technical services may not be enough to guarantee peace and good will on earth. But working together for constructive purposes can create a tendency toward friendly feelings among governments as well as among peoples.

HUMAN RIGHTS

According to the Charter one of the main purposes of the United Nations was "to reaffirm faith in fundamental human rights." In Article 56, also, the Charter lays an obligation on the member states to cooperate with the Organization in promoting universal respect for human rights and freedoms and universal observance of them.

The Charter does not describe in detail what it means by these rights and freedoms. The details were left to be worked out by the Organization.

Defining right and wrong so as to gain the acceptance of more than a hundred different nations is not simple. People of different races and religions in different parts of the world do not agree on some questions—such as, for instance, the rights of women. Moreover, there are differences in the meaning of the word "right"—between the right to a fair trial, for example, and the right to good public health services or to a fair chance to find a job. The different moral aspects of these classes of right have been clearly recognized in the UN debates.

Another point has been clearly recognized. No nation on earth can truly say that it gives its citizens absolute legal justice, on one hand, or absolute protection against poverty and ignorance on the other. But the delegates believed that setting up the best ideals that the majority would agree to would help the world to make progress toward those ideals. Even if the nations could not boast of perfection, they could continue to reaffirm their faith in human rights.

The Universal Declaration of Human Rights

To lay down the general principles of right and wrong the Assembly authorized the Economic and Social Council to appoint a Commission on Human Rights. The Commission was directed to draft a Declaration of Human Rights for adoption by the Assembly. Then in order to bind the nations to give serious attention to these principles, there was to be a Covenant, guaranteeing certain rights of the citizen. Any nation that would ratify the Covenant would be "taking the pledge" to abstain from certain forms of injustice and oppression against its own people.

The Commission was appointed in 1946 with Mrs. Eleanor Roosevelt as chairman and spent two years in discussing how to put into words the great principles of the Declaration. It received advice from many other UN agencies and from outside organizations interested in various aspects of right and wrong.

In general it can be said that all rights that need to be upheld are the opposites of wrongs that someone is suffering. A bill of rights therefore starts with a bill of wrongs that need to be corrected. When the United States Constitution was being adopted some of the states refused to ratify it until they were assured that a Bill of Rights would be added. They wanted a guarantee that the new government would not oppress their people with the same wrongs that had led the colonists to revolt against the British Crown. Thus the United States Constitution forbids the government's forcing the citizens to give house room to soldiers in peacetime, because the British Army had been brutal in this respect in its treatment of colonial families. In the same way the UN Commission studied the common wrongs of the twentieth century in all parts of the world, including ancient, almost prehistoric, horrors revived by Hitler and other totalitarian rulers.

All the wrongs of modern times that were a source of trouble or fear anywhere in the world were raw material for the Commission on Human Rights. The Rights of Man, now as in any previous age, are the right not to suffer the common wrongs of the time.

The Universal Declaration of Human Rights was finally adopted by the Assembly without a dissenting vote on December 10, 1948. The Declaration proclaims the universal right of all persons to life, liberty, and security of person; to freedom from arbitrary arrest; to freedom of movement and residence, of speech, press, assembly, and worship; and to the other legal rights commonly protected by democratic constitutions.

The Declaration also proclaims the rights of people to social security, education, and opportunities to earn a living. These rights are recognized as being in a different class from the legal rights usually described in a constitution. The United Nations makes the distinction between "civil and political" rights on the one hand, and what it calls "economic, social, and cultural" rights on the other. In general, the civil and political rights, if they are stated in the constitution of a country, can be enforced by law. A man who is arbitrarily arrested and held without trial, for instance, can appeal to a court for a fair trial according to law. If the courts are so corrupt or so tainted with dictatorship that the citizen cannot get his constitutional rights, his nation is guilty not only of oppressing the people but also of violating its own laws.

With the economic, social, and cultural rights the situation is different. No country so far has discovered how to give its people full employment under good working conditions all the time. No country knows how to treat its people with moral justice beyond all criticism, nor how to give the people all the education and health that can be desired.

But governments can do much to help in promoting health, education, justice, and prosperity. The weight of world opinion, in fact, stands behind those in any country who would blame the government for unsatisfactory conditions. For example, the Economic and Social Council at its 1950 session decided to discuss the problems of full employment once every year. One obligation of governments, it declared, is to achieve and maintain full employment in an expanding world economy under conditions ensuring fundamental political and economic freedoms to the individual.

In any country, a person who suffers a legal wrong and who can get no redress from the courts is the victim of tyranny or misgovernment. If the democratic voting processes are working fairly well, he and others of like mind may hope to defeat the government in an election and bring in a government that will properly enforce the laws. Or, if the wrongs go so deep that free elections are impossible, those who are wronged will look for opportunities to overthrow the government by violence.

A citizen who is hurt by unemployment or by bad health conditions or other circumstances may blame his government for neglect of its duty. In this class of dispute, the citizen cannot appeal to the courts; for his complaint is only that the government has failed to pass the right laws to help in correcting unemployment or high rates of disease. In democratic countries such forms of discontent ordinarily serve as ammunition for the opposition political parties. If the discontent is sufficient it leads to a change of government at the next election.

Whether the citizen's appeal is to the law or to the political decision in the next election, or, in a dictatorship, to the processes of resistance, in all cases the moral support of the United Nations acts to encourage the citizen in hatred of injustice. Even the most tyrannous governments do not tell their people that the government glories in doing wrong. The arguments are over what is right and what is wrong. When the secret police drag a man away at midnight and send him off to a concentration camp, the government explains that it is protecting the nation against treason. When a dictator holds an election in which the citizens are not allowed a free choice, he does not boast of the wrong; he proclaims his election as the free and democratic choice of the people. But when the Assembly of the United Nations gives its judgment, that judgment has a thundering authority as the voice of mankind. Arbitrary arrest without due process of law is clearly defined and clearly condemned. An election will not be recognized as free and democratic if it is held under oppressive conditions.

The Universal Declaration of Human Rights, therefore, can properly deal with both the duty of nations to treat their people justly, and the duty of nations to serve their people as well as possible in the promotion of health, prosperity, and social security. The Declaration is not a law, but a statement of moral judgment. It is a set of principles to which a nation can appeal in complaining against another nation before the General Assembly. It is also a set of moral standards to which private citizens or political parties can appeal in complaining against the behavior of their own government.

The Covenants

In the Declaration, the Assembly addressed the nations and told them its judgment on the nature of right and wrong. Beyond that, the Assembly directed the Commission on Human Rights to draft a Covenant to be placed before the nations in the form of a treaty to be ratified.

After some discussion the Commission recommended the submission of two Covenants, one covering legal and political rights, and the other economic, social, and cultural rights, since these two kinds of rights are different in their relation to laws and constitutions. This suggestion of dividing the substance of the Declaration into two separate Covenants was accepted by the sixth session of the Assembly in 1951.

A nation ratifying the first Covenant would bind itself to make and enforce laws protecting its own people against unjust and cruel treatment. There is, of course, no enforcement power in the UN to force a nation to keep such a promise—except the power to receive complaints and to proclaim that wrong is being done. Any nation does not lightly put itself in a position to be openly convicted of wrongdoing.

A nation ratifying the second Covenant would acknowledge its duty and responsibility to do all it can to promote better living conditions. In connection with this general duty, it would also recognize certain legal rights connected with economic and social security. The right to join trade unions, for instance, comes in the second Covenant as a necessary economic right to promote the public welfare.

Many democratic countries have constitutional guarantees of some rights that are not included in the UN Covenants. These are rights of historical or local importance that a majority of the delegates did not regard as necessary in a world statement of principles. The Covenants therefore have to provide that ratification will not reduce any rights already established in a ratifying country.

In 1963, the Assembly was still considering the Covenants without arriving at a final form, for many differing cultural and economic traditions, social philosophies, and legal systems must be reconciled before the rights named in the Covenants can be defined and organized into documents that will be internationally acceptable.

In addition to working on the Covenants, the UN is promoting the principles of human rights in various other ways. The 1950 session of the General Assembly, for instance, proclaimed December 10 as Human Rights Day. This anniversary is celebrated in many countries with ceremonies to remind the people of the Declaration and to spread the knowledge of its principles. The UN actions on a number of special problems also serve to illustrate and buttress the general principles of the Declaration.

Freedom of the News

One of the most complex rights is that of freedom to give and receive the news. A UN conference on this subject, held in the spring of 1948 in Geneva, adopted three draft conventions: one on gathering and sending of news, one on the right of governments to demand correction of news that they claim to be false, and one on freedom of information.

The first of these proposals would ask the nations to agree that foreign newsmen could have the same right to get at the sources of news as the native newsgatherers. The second convention, on the right of correction, would bind all governments agreeing to it that whenever a news source in any country gives out any item that is objectionable to another member of the agreement, the offended country can send an official complaint to the government of the country where the story originated. Then the government receiving the complaint promises to give it due publicity. This convention came into effect on August 24, 1962.

The third convention deals with freedom of information, a subject complicated by the fact that it includes on one side the freedom of newsmen and publishers to get and give out the news, on another side the freedom of the people to read or hear the news, and on a third side the rights of governments to protect themselves. The right of publication is easily corrupted into the publication of false reports. The rights of government are easily corrupted into censorship and the "big lie" techniques of public deception. The simple purpose of UN action might be to protect the public's right to full and honest news; but there are some governments that are not ready to grant the public any such right without reservations. The result is that the moral authority of the UN in this matter is less certain in its pronouncements than in dealing with other rights.

Genocide

Genocide is the subject of a special convention adopted on December 9, 1948, by the General Assembly and submitted to the members for ratification. The ratifying states agree that the crime of genocide consists of trying to destroy a "national, ethnical, racial, or religious group as such." Genocidal actions include killing members of a group because they are members, causing them serious injury in body or mind, or trying to destroy the group by preventing births among its members or by transferring its children to other groups. The ratifying states agree to the punishment of any of their citizens who commit genocide, including public officials responsible for genocidal policies.

Of course, a state seriously determined to practice genocide might not hesitate to deny all the facts, whether it had signed the convention or not. But the convention helps to bring to a focus the force of world opinion, which even dictators are not entirely able to disregard.

In 1955 the General Assembly organized a system of education in human rights. Fellowships and scholarships are granted. Seminars have been held on such subjects as

"Protection of human rights in criminal law and procedure," "Judicial and other remedies against the illegal exercise or abuse of administrative authority," and "The status of women in family life." In 1956 the Economic and Social Council established a reporting schedule under which all UN members are asked to report every three years, telling what progress they have made in human rights protection.

Rights of Women

The Economic and Social Council established a Commission on the Status of Women in June, 1946. This Commission deals with the political and legal rights of women, and such matters as equal opportunity in education and employment.

The Assembly adopted a Convention on the Political Rights of Women on December 20, 1952, and submitted it to the member nations for their ratification. Any nation joining in this convention admits the right of women to vote, to hold public office, and to serve on public institutions, such as juries, without discrimination. In some countries the laws do not grant these rights to women and would have to be changed before the government could become a party to the convention.

In 1957 the Assembly adopted a convention on the nationality of married women, which provides that in states adhering to this convention a woman who marries a man of differing nationality shall not necessarily have to take his nationality. In addition her nationality would not be automatically affected by divorce or by her husband changing his own.

Another convention, adopted in 1962, provides that states party to it shall establish a minimum age for marriage, require the registration of all marriages, and permit no marriage without the free consent of both parties.

The Commission receives yearly reports on the status of women in the dependent territories and has recommended that UN missions sent to inspect conditions in these territories include women members as well as men, so as to promote equal rights of women there.

The Commission has made detailed studies of marriage

laws and customs in different countries, and in 1960 it
adopted a draft of a convention designed to prevent
various ancient practices, such as polygamy or marriage of
children. Other subjects of study include a number of
inequalities in the position of women in various countries,
which will not be easily or quickly changed. One of these
is the difference in opportunity for employment in the
public service. Another is unequal pay for women doing
equal work with men. Another is the unequal position between men and women in the holding of family property
and in other legal features of the family relationship. Still
another is the unequal opportunity in most countries for
women to get an education. All these will require long
discussion, which in itself will create pressures toward more
equal treatment of women in many countries.

Rights of the Child

The Declaration of Geneva, adopted on September 26,
1924, by the League of Nations, set forth the rights of
the child, and served as the inspiration for a similar action by the United Nations. In 1946 the Social Commission
and the Commission on Human Rights were given the
responsibility of drafting a new Declaration, which was
unanimously adopted by the General Assembly on November 20, 1959.

The Declaration of the Rights of the Child proclaims
that every child on earth should have special protection
and opportunity to develop in a healthy and normal manner in conditions of freedom and dignity, to have a name
and a nationality, and to have proper food, shelter, rec-
reation, and medical attention. He should be given special
care if he is handicapped, or in time of disaster; he should
be protected from cruelty and exploitation and from any
form of discrimination. Finally, the child should be brought
up "in a spirit of understanding, tolerance, friendship
among peoples, peace, and universal brotherhood."

Prevention of Discrimination

The Commission on Human Rights has a Subcommission on the Prevention of Discrimination and Protection

of Minorities, which has made a series of worldwide studies on various kinds of wrongs done to minorities. A report on discrimination in education, presented in 1957, was taken over for follow-up by UNESCO. The second, on discrimination in employment, was taken up by ILO. A report on religious discrimination and oppression was issued in January, 1960.

This report stated that oppression on account of religion had been dying out, but that new outbursts of racial and religious hostility in various parts of the world were ominous, and the trend toward religious tolerance might be reversed. The report proposed a set of rules that should be recommended for the guidance of the nations, to prevent oppression in regard to the right to keep or change religion, and to show religion or belief, particularly by different forms of worship; pilgrimages; methods of disposal of the dead; religious holidays; dietary practices; marriage rites; religious training; the taking of an oath; conscientious objection to military service; and secrecy of information given in confidence to a cleric.

Other forms of discrimination studied by the Subcommission have included the denial of political rights and of the right of a citizen to leave any country, including his own, and return freely to his own country.

War Victims

Prisoners of war and refugees have presented a heartbreaking situation since the beginning of World War II.

Millions of men, women, and children disappeared without trace in the course of the war. Some of them are alive, and those who are lucky may still be reunited with their surviving relatives. Most of the missing persons are dead, but there are no records of their deaths. One of the results of these disappearances is to tangle the legal titles to property. The heirs cannot get a clear title. Another is that the wife or husband of a missing person may not be permitted to remarry without positive proof of death.

The Economic and Social Council brought up the subject of the missing-persons problem in 1948. As a result the Assembly called a special conference of governments at UN Headquarters in March, 1950, which set up a Convention on the Declaration of Death of Missing Persons. The Convention provides for a bureau that will examine such evidence as may be obtainable. When it finds no reason to the contrary it will declare a missing person dead, for purposes of fixing the legal position of his survivors.

Refugees

Another large-scale problem left over from World War II was that of the refugees. The International Refugee Organization, which was formed by a number of governments to take care of the war refugees, was dissolved in 1949, leaving the remaining part of the burden to be taken up by the United Nations. The Office of the United Nations High Commissioner for Refugees began operations on January 1, 1951.

The High Commissioner's office was made responsible for the interests of most of the people in the world who have fled from their home countries and dare not go back for fear of persecution. Exceptions are refugees who have been given national rights in the country where they now are, and some others, such as Palestinian Arabs, who have a special agency looking after them.

The UN pays only for the expense of running the Office of the High Commissioner and its various branches, a total of less than a million dollars a year. The expense of taking care of the refugees is paid for from voluntary contributions, public and private.

The High Commissioner is responsible for the international protection of refugees, the promotion of activities that will help the refugees to find secure homes, and the coordination of private organizations that work for refugees. International protection is necessary because the laws of most countries have no place for foreigners without passports or other evidence that they belong somewhere. A "stateless" person may be refused the right to enter a country at all.

Accordingly, the refugee problem has stimulated international action to define the legal position of people without a country. A Convention Relating to the Status of Refugees was adopted in 1951 at a Conference of Plenipotentiaries held in Geneva. By 1960 it had been signed by seventy states. This convention is designed to make clear what people are refugees and what rights they shall have. Other international agreements provide for the settlement of refugees in the countries where they are living, and for giving refugees the benefit of social security and medical assistance. The High Commissioner has the authority under a General Assembly resolution to make agreements with governments to improve the condition of refugees.

In addition to the remaining World War II refugees in Europe, and those who escaped from Hungary in 1956, in 1963 the High Commissioner had serious refugee problems in Asia and Africa. In Asia there are escapees from Communist China, mainly in Hong Kong, and from Tibet in India and Pakistan. In Africa the thousands who fled from Algeria when it was at war with France were being brought home and resettled, but there are still displaced people in southern Africa from the Portuguese colonies and other disturbed areas.

Altogether, in 1963 some 1,400,000 persons were under the High Commissioner's protection.

Race Conflicts in South Africa

In the first session of the Assembly, in 1946, India complained about the treatment of Indians in the Union of South Africa. One of India's chief accusations was that the Land Tenure and Representation Act of 1946 forced the segregation of Indians in both living quarters and in business.

India said the situation was likely to cause unfriendly feelings between the two countries, and that it violated a treaty and the UN Charter. South Africa replied that segregation was a domestic question which the UN had no right to meddle with, and that the agreement quoted by India was not a treaty. South Africa also pointed out that the UN Charter mentioned human rights but did not say what they were, and that until there was a UN bill of rights, telling just what rights were included, the UN could not find anyone in violation of the Charter on that score.

The Assembly rejected a South African proposal to ask the International Court of Justice whether this matter was purely domestic. Instead, the Assembly said that friendly relations between two member states were plainly being impaired. It advised South Africa to conform with the previous agreement and with the Charter.

In its seventh session, in 1952, the Assembly found the dispute no nearer to a settlement. Meanwhile thirteen Asian states, ranging from Lebanon to the Philippines, brought in a complaint against the South African policy known as *apartheid,* for segregating the Negroes. The Assembly set up a three-man commission to study the race situation in South Africa. It also passed a resolution declaring that where several races live together in a country they ought to be equal before the law. The Assembly affirmed that racial discrimination was contrary to the pledges of the members who had signed the Charter, and solemnly called on all members to conform to their Charter obligations. South Africa refused to accept these resolutions.

In 1959 the Assembly still found South Africa refusing to change its policies. On apartheid, a resolution expressing disapproval and deep concern was passed by a vote of 62 to 3, with 7 abstaining. The delegates who did not vote for the resolution declared that their governments were opposed to race segregation, but that they regarded apartheid as a domestic policy of South Africa, in which the UN had no authority to interfere. But the vast majority of the nations consider that oppression in any part of the world is a blot on civilization and in the long run a danger to peace, and therefore a matter of concern to the nations assembled in the UN. Moreover, the troubles in South Africa are becoming more dangerous as more and more new independent nations, governed by the native peoples, are established on that continent.

South Africa has, of course, the legal power to defy the opinion of the United Nations. But the moral pressure goes on increasing with the passage of time. South Africans who support their government's white-supremacy laws cannot escape the knowledge that the world regards their country with disapproval and distaste.

The fact that the power of the General Assembly is moral rather than legislative or military has made it increasingly hard for wrongdoing nations to persuade the

Assembly that it has no legal right to discuss any and all moral questions and to pass judgment on what the member governments do to their own people. This development tends to make hard the way of the transgressor, and apparently it will continue to do so.

By May of 1964 the racial tensions in South Africa had seriously increased. New legislation had tightened the system of race discrimination. A UN Special Committee on Apartheid was particularly concerned with the trials of Negro leaders, in which several had already been condemned to death. In a report submitted to the Assembly and the Security Council the Committee urged that the UN impose economic sanctions to force South Africa to grant freedom to political prisoners opposing apartheid.

In reply, the South African representative said that the three men condemned to death had been convicted of murdering a witness who might have appeared against them in their trial for sabotage. It was evident that the stage was set for increasing violence and suppression of resistance to the Government's policies.

Slavery

In 1947, the American Federation of Labor asked the United Nations to make a complete study of forced labor in all member states and to take action to get rid of it.

The Economic and Social Council received the A. F. of L. request and invited the International Labor Organization and the Secretary-General to study the problem. In 1951 the Council adopted a proposal, put forward by Britain and the United States, to set up a committee of inquiry. The committee was told to study "systems of forced or corrective labor which are employed as a means of political coercion or punishment for holding or expressing political views."

The committee sent a questionnaire to all states, whether members of the UN, of the ILO, or of neither. It also invited all private organizations with information on forced labor to come in and testify. Most of the countries of the world replied to the committee's questionnaire, and a number of organizations and private persons gave evidence. The committee decided to send out to all the interested governments a summary of the testimony. It reported to the Assembly that the Soviet Union and the states associated with it employed forced labor on an extensive scale.

In September, 1956, a UN conference in Geneva adopted an antislavery agreement, bringing up to date a League of Nations agreement of 1926. The new treaty goes beyond the well-known kinds of slavery to forbid such things as debt bondage, serfdom, bride price, inheritance of wives, and certain abuses in the adoption of children.

It is worth noting that the practice of employing convicts in a prison factory or on highway construction, as is done in many civilized countries, was not the target of the "forced labor" investigation, which applied only to the punishment of *political* prisoners. Merciful treatment of criminals is also important as a matter of human rights, but is not in the same classification with the problem of political slave camps.

In 1957 the International Labor Conference further defined the unallowable forms of forced labor. In addition to its use as punishment for political activity, it was also condemned as a method for mobilizing labor for economic development, as in Communist China; as punishment for taking part in strikes; and as a means of racial, social, or religious discrimination.

The duty of governments to protect their people from epidemic diseases, economic depressions, and widespread ignorance, can no longer be denied. But this duty has only recently been recognized and governments are slow to shake off old ways and take on new responsibilities. The United Nations helps to push the nations along the way they must go to find better conditions of life for their people.

The moral pressure of the United Nations—pressure on reluctant nations to give up legal wrongs—is a striking example of the power of united action. The advance of justice and mercy can often be pushed with the greatest effect by the moral pressure of people not injured themselves but shocked by cruelty to others. Wrongdoers are extremely sensitive to condemnation by the "public"—that is, by the people whose disapproval may be injurious to their success. This sensitivity of nations is constantly proved in the meetings of the UN Assembly and the Security Council. No nation boasts of wrongdoing; if a nation is determined to do evil it looks for ways to evade the judgment of the world.

When an overwhelming majority of the Assembly, made up of delegates of many races, religions, and languages, passes judgment, there is no more formidable judgment to be had on earth.

NON-SELF-GOVERNING PEOPLES

The age of modern European imperialism began with the opening of sea routes from Europe to Asia around the Cape of Good Hope and to America across the Atlantic. After A.D. 1500 most of the world came under European control. Then came a movement for independence, starting in the eighteenth century with the successful revolt of thirteen British colonies on the North American coast, and continuing with the Spanish colonies in Central and South America. The movement for independence, called "self-determination" by Woodrow Wilson at Versailles in 1919, has now progressed so far that the the United Nations Assembly treats it as a matter of course.

In the UN there are two systems under which the nations that govern dependent territories give an accounting of how they treat their subject peoples. One is known as Trusteeship, under which the governing nations report to the UN Trusteeship Council. In the other, less formal system, the nations report to the Secretary-General on the economic, social, and educational conditions in their areas.

Trusteeship

The trusteeship system has come down from the mandate system of the League of Nations. After World War I, the former German colonies were taken over by the League. Their administration was farmed out to various Powers which accepted a "mandate" to govern in the interest of the people and to give account of their stewardship to the League. These areas became "trust territories" under the United Nations by agreement with the various Powers that accepted responsibility for administering them.

In July, 1959, there were ten UN trust territories, all originally League of Nations mandates except Somaliland, which was taken from Italy in World War II. They were: in East Africa—Ruanda-Urundi, administered by Belgium; Somaliland, administered by Italy; and Tanganyika, administered by the United Kingdom. In West Africa— the Cameroons, administered by France; the Cameroons administered by the United Kingdom; and Togoland, administered by France. In the Pacific area—Nauru, administered by Australia, on behalf of Australia, New Zealand, and the United Kingdom; New Guinea, administered by Australia; Western Samoa, administered by New Zealand; and the Trust Territory of the Pacific Islands, administered by the United States.

The UN Charter established a Trusteeship Council to look after the interests of the people in the trust territories. On the Council are all the UN members that hold trusteeships and an equal number of other members.

The Trust Territory of the Pacific Islands has been specially designated a "strategic area," and the trusteeship agreement provides that certain sections of it may be closed for reasons of military security. The Trusteeship Council submits reports on this area to the Security Council instead of to the Assembly.

The Council sends out a questionnaire of several hundred detailed questions on the political, economic, social, and educational progress of the trust territories. It also receives hundreds of petitions and complaints from organizations and individual people in the territories.

Most of the petitions are on political matters; others complain of poor schools and health services, racial discrimination, or land tenure problems. Prominent leaders appear sometimes as petitioners before the Council and later, after their country becomes independent, reappear in the news as President or Prime Minister. This direct right of access to the UN by leaders of subject people is an important feature of the trusteeship system.

The Council sends regular missions to visit every trust

territory once every few years. The missions are chosen from a wide variety of nations to get a broad view of the problems. For instance, one mission to West Africa had representatives of Iraq, Belgium, Mexico, and the United States. The missions look over the territory, talk with the people, and are ready to hear comments and complaints.

The trustee government is required to submit a full report every year. It sends a special representative prepared to answer questions about the territory. On the basis of all the various sources of information, the Council makes a report on each trust territory to the General Assembly.

The General Assembly in turn discusses the trusteeship reports and makes recommendations for the government of the territories. It does not hesitate to criticize what has been done and to call for more education, better laws, and more signs of progress toward self-government.

Togoland

The Trusteeship Council and the Assembly take a keen interest in old customs that may have been long established in a territory but which offend the moral sense of outsiders. The British Administration in Togoland on the West Coast of Africa, for instance, was asked not only to provide more schools and medical services, but also to abolish corporal punishment. The Administration proudly reported in 1953 that during the previous year a well-equipped hospital was established in the territory, free primary schools were opened, and a new secondary school and two teacher-training colleges were established; and finally, that during the year no court in the territory had sentenced anyone to be whipped. The Council urged the Administration to continue its efforts for the complete removal of corporal punishment from the territorial law.

In 1954 the General Assembly again discussed the Togoland problems at length. Britain called attention to the fact that it was administering British Togoland in conjunction with the adjoining Gold Coast territory. As the Gold Coast was soon to be granted independence, the British wished to drop the Togoland trusteeship.

Representatives from the area indicated a wide divergence of opinion. Some wanted to unite British Togoland with the new independent Gold Coast; others wanted union with French Togoland.

Finally, in 1956, the people of British Togoland were invited to vote on whether to join the Gold Coast in setting up the new state of Ghana, or to continue under British administration pending some other solution of their problems. The voting was orderly and the people voted 93,000 to 67,000 to join the Gold Coast. Accordingly, the territory is now a part of the state of Ghana, which was admitted in 1957 to the United Nations as the eighty-first member.

As for French Togoland, a special UN Commission reported to the Trusteeship Council in September, 1957, that the relations between France and the territory had been much improved by a new governing statute, passed by the French Parliament in the middle of 1956 and endorsed by the votes of over 70 percent of the Togoland people in October of that year. The new statute gave wide powers to the Togoland Government, reserving to the French authorities only the administrative jobs considered to be "financially and technically onerous." The Commission regarded these jobs as likely to be transferred gradually as local people were trained to take over the more difficult kinds of work. The Trusteeship Council commended the French Administration and sent the report along to the Assembly "in order to set in motion the influences that would help to bring further progress toward self-government."

In April, 1958, elections for a new legislature were held under UN supervision. More than 400,000 people voted. After the election the French and Togolese governments agreed that the country would become independent on April 27, 1960, and the General Assembly voting in November, 1958, unanimously endorsed the plan for independence.

The French Cameroons, another trust territory in Africa, also chose independence through a vote of its elected legislature in October, 1958, with the consent of the French authority, to become effective January 1, 1960. The General Assembly, after examining the report of a visiting mission on conditions in the territory, voted to end the trusteeship on that date and recommended that the new nation should be admitted to UN membership on becoming independent. This was accomplished on September 20, 1960.

In the British Cameroons, on the other hand, there was much doubt as to what the people wanted. The territory was administered with Nigeria, which was scheduled for independence in October, 1960. As the sentiments in the northern and southern parts of the country were evidently not alike, the Assembly provided first for a vote in the northern section, on whether to join Nigeria or to put off the decision until some later date. The people voted in November, 1959, and chose to postpone the decision, by a vote of 113,859 to 70,546, with only 525 votes thrown out as invalid.

The vote in the southern section, however, was deferred because the Assembly became convinced that the issues had not yet become clear enough to obtain a useful decision.

New votes were held in February, 1961, as a result of which the Northern Cameroons joined the Federation of Nigeria, and the Southern Cameroons joined the Republic of Cameroon, formerly under French Administration.

These situations illustrate how the UN purpose of extending self-government to dependent peoples can be peacefully carried out wherever the governing powers are willing and ready to agree.

Somalia

Another good example of how the UN promotes independence is Somalia, formerly Somaliland, an independent nation since July, 1960. This Italian colony was taken by the British in the last war, and its future was left to the decision of the United Nations. The Assembly decided in 1949 that the Somalis were not ready for independence but might be after ten years of development. Italy was appointed as Trustee, with a special Advisory Council of representatives from Egypt, Colombia, and the Philippines to aid it in its administration. The British turned over the government to the new administration on April 1, 1950.

The Somalis had a hard road to travel before they could

expect to stand on their own feet as an independent nation. A population of 1,200,000, made up chiefly of nomadic shepherds roaming over a largely arid territory, they would need to find ways of increasing their earning power, especially in foreign trade. In order for many of them to settle down they would need to tap the groundwater with an extensive system of wells.

They also would have to learn to read and write, not merely in Italian but in their own tongue. That presented a problem, for there was no written Somali language and the spoken language was divided into many dialects. Two language experts from UNESCO were called to advise the Administration on what form of Somali to make official, and to invent an alphabet in which to write it.

Politically, there were already some definite signs of life. For example, there was the Somali Youth League, strongly anti-Italian, which had been founded in 1943. The Youth League representative told the Trusteeship Council in 1953 that the Administration was moving too slowly. He demanded an over-all economic plan and a native legislature with the right to legislate.

Another representative advised the Council not to be too much in a hurry for political democracy. He said:

The tribes cannot be disbanded and a new system substituted in a few years. They must be guided and interested by means of appropriate measures so that a gradual transformation takes place until final social, economic, and political progress has penetrated and extended to the entire Territory, creating new living conditions. Somaliland's evolution will be the result of two concurrent movements: first, the development of the parties and of the various administrative and political organizations which the Administering Authority is establishing, particularly in the cities and other centers; secondly, the evolution of the tribes as a result of a diffusion of new ideas and above all of changes in the economic situation.

Despite all the obstacles, the Somalis made good progress in their ten-year training period. The Assembly had decided that Somalia would become independent by December 2, 1960. But the Administration and the new Somali Government reported that the country would be ready by July 1, and the Assembly voted to end the trusteeship on that date.

Western Samoa

In November, 1946, Western Samoa was being shifted from a League of Nations mandate to a United Nations trusteeship, under New Zealand as administering Power. The Administrator invited the inhabitants to express their opinions on the proposed trusteeship agreement that New Zealand had submitted to the UN.

The Samoans petitioned for immediate self-government under the protection of New Zealand. At the suggestion of New Zealand, the Trusteeship Council decided to send a mission to Western Samoa. The mission was made up of members from Belgium, Chile, and the United States. It was in Samoa in July and August, 1947, and at the same time the New Zealand Government consulted with the Samoans. In November, New Zealand adopted a new form of government for Western Samoa which was closely in line with the mission's recommendations.

Under the new Samoan Amendment Act, the principal chiefs were established with the High Commissioner in a Council of State. Samoan members had a majority in the Legislature, with authority to make the laws and to dispose of the revenues of the territory. The Trusteeship Council expressed satisfaction with the New Zealand policies and recommended that the Samoans should take on more and more of the responsibilities of self-government.

In 1959 the Trusteeship Council again sent a mission to Western Samoa, and on hearing its report endorsed the New Zealand plan for political development of the territory leading to independence. Western Samoa became independent on January 1, 1962.

Tanganyika

A notable feature of the British trusteeship in Tanganyika was the report of the visiting mission in 1960 calling attention to "the peaceful and harmonious atmosphere of good will." In this atmosphere the British and Tanganyikan governments agreed to the independence of the country, which was established on December 9, 1961.

The right of the UN to send missions to look over the trust territories was new. This right did not exist under the League of Nations mandate system. The trusteeship system is considerably broader in its scope and gives the administration of these territories a much more extensive supervision than under the League.

By 1963, only three territories were left under trusteeship: Nauru, New Guinea, and the Pacific Islands Trust Territory.

Non-Self-Governing Territories

The trust territories represent the direct responsibility of the UN, being in each case the ex-colonies of defeated Powers whose sovereign claims were wiped out by war. As for the other territories, ranked as non-self-governing, the UN Charter lays an obligation on the Powers that control them to report on their progress each year. Many of these territories have a considerable range of freedom in local affairs, although their foreign relations are decided by the metropolitan Power. Others are governed by administrations in which the inhabitants have little or no part.

Information on the progress of non-self-governing territories is sent to the Secretary-General of the UN, who submits it to a special committee for study. It then goes to the Assembly for action. In the Charter the governing countries agreed to send information on only social, educational, and economic conditions in their territories. But the Assembly has repeatedly asked them to report also on the development of self-governing institutions.

In 1961 the United Kingdom, which controls more than half of the remaining non-self-governing territories, notified the General Assembly that in the future it would supply information on political and constitutional progress in its forty-two territories, and the information was supplied in 1963.

In cases where a nation stops sending information the

Assembly calls for an explanation of what change has justified erasing the name of a territory from the non-self-governing list. An example was when the United States ratified the Constitution of Puerto Rico, which gave that country the right to choose all its public officials and make its own laws. The United States then classified Puerto Rico as "self-governing" and ceased to report on it to the UN. The Assembly voted to accept the claim that Puerto Rico is self-governing, with the Latin-American countries voting "Aye." Similarly, U. S. reports on Alaska and Hawaii were dropped when they became states of the Union.

The Assembly has passed resolutions advising the governing nations to apply the principles of the Declaration of Human Rights to the people of dependent areas, and to take advantage of technical assistance opportunities for developing those areas. Reports on such action are requested.

Libya

The United Nations, representing the world community, is the natural sponsor for any new nation asking to be born. Korea and Somalia are not the only UN godchildren. Another former Italian colony, Libya, was judged to be politically ready for early independence although it would need technical and economic help in getting established. In November, 1949, the Assembly appointed a commissioner, Adrian Pelt of the Netherlands, as head of an international council to help the Libyans set up a government. The Council met on April 25, 1950, and by December 2 of the same year a Libyan National Assembly had been organized and had chosen the Emir of Cyrenaica as king. A provisional federal government was established in March, 1951, and on December 24 King Idris I proclaimed Libya's independence. The UN General Assembly welcomed the new nation, but it was not admitted to the UN because of a Soviet veto until the "package deal" of 1955.

Foreign help to Libya came from various sources. Financial help came from Britain, France, Italy, and Turkey. Technical assistance was given in a cooperative program of the United Nations and the United States Point Four.

The country started as one of the poorest in the world, but not without hope of improvement. The average income was the equivalent of about $35 per person per year. Eighty-five percent of the people were unable to read or write, and three hundred infants out of every thousand died before they were a year old. There were no resources except a generally poor soil, a scanty supply of water, and a population largely untrained but with ability to learn and an ambition to improve their way of living.

Most of the work therefore started with education and training. UNESCO gave technical help in starting new schools, and especially in the training of teachers. Students took training in all sorts of needed skills, from typing and bookkeeping to Arabic and English, geography, carpentry, and mechanical drawing. In the oases of the Fezzan a UNESCO expert from Austria organized education centers to teach the people reading and the use of better tools and better methods of hygiene. A team of olive pruners from Tunisia traveled throughout the country showing how to prune the olive trees so as to get better crops. Sheep were improved by importing better breeding stock from Turkey.

By 1956 Libya was reported to have one of the fastest-growing school systems in the world. Developments in these early years included a successful community center for women in the Fezzan, improvements in vegetable growing as a result of demonstration gardens, and establishment of many literacy centers that soon grew into community clubs. There was also a rapid spread of football and volleyball in the country.

Meanwhile WHO set up a program of public health, and the Libyan Government made a contract with UNICEF to test and vaccinate the children against tuberculosis. An expert from the World Meteorological Organization organized a system of weather reports, important not only for flying but also for modern agriculture. Foreign experts in government helped the new Libyan Administration to set up its necessary public services with a modern budget and tax system and sound foreign trade and banking policies.

In 1959 the World Bank, at the Libyan Government's request, sent a mission to Libya, to survey the economic

104 THE UNITED NATIONS AND HOW IT WORKS

situation and help work out a development program. In 1960 the UN Special Fund agreed to contribute $1,000,-000 over a five-year period for an Institute of Higher Technology in Tripoli. The Institute offers four-year courses in civil, mechanical, and electrial engineering, and in food processing.

One might get the impression that there is not much room for Libyan independence. But in fact, every foreign expert came to Libya because the Government invited his organization to send him. The Libyans have been working hard to push back the desert and build themselves a prosperous country, using all the expert advice they could get.

South West Africa

This former German colony was mandated to South Africa by the League of Nations after World War I. It became a serious problem in 1946, when South Africa refused to transfer it to a trusteeship under the UN like the other mandated territories. South Africa took the position that with the death of the League of Nations, the mandate ceased to exist, and that the administering Power was no longer responsible to any outside authority. The United Nations has never accepted this position.

In 1949 the General Assembly asked the International Court to give a ruling on the South West Africa question. In 1950 the Court ruled that South Africa still has international obligations in connection with the territory, according to the Covenant of the League of Nations and the terms of its mandate, and that the right to supervise the administration of the territory now rests in the United Nations, to which reports and petitions should be submitted. The Court declared that South Africa had no right to govern South West Africa if acting alone but only if acting with the consent of the United Nations.

By 1959 the South African delegation at the UN was at least taking part in the discussions, but the report of the UN Committee on South West Africa was not encouraging. The Committee said it was "particularly disturbed" by the spread of racial segregation and the plans for mass removal of the native peoples from their ancestral lands to make room for European settlement.

During the debate over the Committee's findings, a number of petitioners were heard, despite strong opposition of the South African delegation. The burden of the testimony was that the native people were suffering desperately low living standards and working under conditions of "near slavery." The Government was imposing segregation, cruel punishments, and a system of migratory labor by which families and the traditional social order had been broken up. The petitioners charged that South Africa was planning to annex the country.

A member of the South African parliament spoke on the economic problems of the territory and the efforts that his country was making to build highways and railroads, and to provide dams and wells to help out the meager water supply. He also stated that there were 35,000 non-European pupils in schools, as compared with only 2,430 in 1922. The South African Foreign Minister took part in the debate, describing his country's policy, which remained one of firm refusal to make any formal agreement granting the United Nations the right to supervise the administration of South West Africa. But he gave assurances that "the door will be left open" for further discussions.

In 1961 the General Assembly proclaimed the "inalienable right of the people of South West Africa to independence and national sovereignty." It appointed a Special Committee of twenty-four members to make arrangements with the Government of South Africa for establishing the independence of South West Africa, and also asked this committee to take over the reporting work of the previous committee.

The Chairman and Vice-Chairman of the Special Committee visited South Africa in 1962 and held discussions both with government officials and with many private persons representing various elements in the population. The General Assembly, after hearing a report of these discussions, passed resolutions condemning the refusal of South Africa to cooperate, and urging member states to "take into consideration the anxieties" of many members over the sale of arms to South Africa. In the 1963 Assembly, further resolutions declared the right of South West Africa to independence, and pointed out that any attempt by South Africa to annex any part of it would be an act of aggression. The Assembly called the Security Council's attention to the dangerous situation there, and decided to keep the question of South West Africa on its agenda as requiring constant and urgent attention.

In May, 1964, the Special Committee discussed with grave concern the proposals of a South African Commission of Inquiry, known as the Odendaal Commission, which had recommended a policy of separating South West Africa into areas reserved exclusively for whites and for nonwhites. This policy would be an extension of the South African plan of apartheid into the mandated territory, and was regarded by most of the committee members as a further step toward annexation of the territory. Since the South African Government had announced that it would postpone action on the new scheme until the World Court had ruled on a case brought before it by Ethiopia and Liberia concerning the situation of South West Africa, there was some disagreement as to what immediate action the Committee should take. The majority, however, voted for a strong resolution condemning the Odendaal proposals and calling the case to the attention of the Security Council as a threat to peace and security.

West Irian

When Indonesia became independent in December, 1949, the Dutch colonial territory of West New Guinea (West Irian) was not included in the new nation. The Indonesians claimed this territory as a rightful part of their country. The Dutch position was that the New Guinea tribes were culturally quite different from the Indonesians and would be treated as an oppressed minority, whereas under Netherlands Administration they could be suitably prepared and in due time become self-governing. The General Assembly discussed this problem from 1954 to 1957 and again in 1961.

The Netherlands proposed in November, 1961, that the inhabitants be asked to vote on which government they preferred, but Indonesia refused, saying that West Irian was a part of Indonesia and the question of independence could not be considered.

In December, 1961, there was fighting in the disputed area between the Dutch and the Indonesians. The Secretary-General urged both governments to instruct their representatives at the UN to discuss with him the possibilities of an accord. The result was an agreement to transfer the administration of the colony to Indonesia, but with an obligation of Indonesia's part to give the population a free choice as to their own future before the end of 1969. By a resolution passed on September 21, 1962, the General Assembly assumed the obligation of doing its part in carrying out the terms of this agreement when the time comes for Indonesia to fulfill its promise.

Meanwhile a UN Temporary Executive Authority was given the responsibility of administering the colony. The UN team was made up of UN civil servants from thirty-two different nations. The UN Authority transferred the administration to Indonesia on May 1, 1963.

Portuguese Colonies

In view of numerous complaints about Portugal's treatment of her colonies, particularly Angola, and the testimony of refugees, the UN has been increasingly concerned. From the first Portugal has refused to report on these colonies as non-self-governing, saying that they are overseas provinces with the same rights as the home provinces of Portugal itself.

Since the UN freely agrees that Alaska and Hawaii are self-governing states of the United States, this presented a problem: how could Portugal's overseas provinces be technically distinguished from those of the United States? In 1955 the Assembly appointed a committee to discuss the question. The committee held that the Charter rule applied to territories "known to be of the colonial type," and particularly those that are geographically separated and different by race or culture from the administering country. Undoubtedly, the reason that this definition does not apply to Puerto Rico is that it is not known to be of the colonial type because the majority of Puerto Ricans do not so regard it. If they were to resist like the Angolans, the UN would class them as oppressed.

In 1961 the Assembly set up a Special Committee on Territories under Portuguese Administration. The Committee reported in 1962 a deep feeling of dissatisfaction and tension among the people, caused by poor public services and forcible suppression of all political activities looking toward independence. It also reported that arms supplied to Portugal for defense, by her allies in the North Atlantic Treaty Organization, had been diverted to the suppression of the colonial peoples.

The Assembly adopted a resolution in December, 1962, condemning the actions of the Portuguese Government, requesting other nations not to supply arms to Portugal, and requesting the Security Council to "take all appropriate measures" to secure Portugal's compliance with UN demands.

The Assembly also decided to establish a training program for the people of the Portuguese colonies, in preparation for independence, since Portugal had failed to do so.

Declaration on the Granting of Independence to Colonial Countries and Peoples

After World War II most of the large colonial areas such as India, Indonesia, and most of Africa, which had previously been governed by the European Powers, became independent—sometimes after armed revolt, but often with cordial good will on both sides. The Philippine Islands, for instance, long promised independence by the United States, were launched with good will in 1946. However, numerous smaller areas, most of them islands, remained under the control of the Great Powers.

The long struggle against colonialism had left bitter feelings in many parts of Asia and Africa. In 1960 these sentiments led to the passage by the UN General Assembly of a Declaration calling for the total abolition of colonial rule. The Declaration stated that alien domination is a denial of human rights, is contrary to the UN Charter, and is an impediment to the promotion of world peace. Further, all peoples have the right to self-determination, to freely determine their political status and their economic, social, and cultural development.

"Inadequacy of political, economic, social or educational preparedness should never serve as a pretext for delaying independence. . . . All armed action or repressive measures . . . shall cease . . . ," and immediate steps shall be taken to transfer all powers, without any conditions or reservations, in order to enable the people to enjoy complete independence and freedom.

Finally, any attempt to disrupt the national unity and the traditional integrity of a country is incompatible with the UN Charter.

In 1961 the Assembly noted with distress that about sixty territories were still under foreign rule, and appointed a Special Committee of twenty-four members to study the application of the Declaration and to make recommendations to the administering Powers on how to liberate their territories. During 1962 the Committee considered some twelve territories under Portuguese and British rule, nearly all of them in Eastern Africa. The Portuguese colonies, as previously noted, presented the most acute cases of suppression and disorder.

In a discussion between the Portuguese Government and representatives of the African states, organized by the Secretary-General in 1963, the Foreign Minister of Portugal explained his government's understanding of "self-determination." Essentially it meant self-government, with equal voting rights for the colonials and equal representation in the government of Portugal—which is, after all, a dictatorship. The Africans objected to the fact that the Portuguese definition of self-determination did not include the right of the people of a colony to decide to break all ties with Lisbon and set up as an independent sovereign state.

This question is more complex than it looks at first sight.

If the territories are, as claimed by Portugal, really an "integral" part of the Portuguese nation, it is generally accepted that the central government has a right to refuse to let them break off and set up for themselves. Most of the world regards the Portuguese colonies as colonies, not as integral parts of Portugal. The important word is "integral," which involves geography, race, language, and culture, and partly, but not absolutely, the wishes of the inhabitants. The United States has decided to treat Hawaii and Alaska as integral, despite geographical separation and racial differences, while the Philippines and Puerto Rico were treated as not integral, and were therefore free to choose independence if they wanted it. Few people have disagreed with these particular decisions.

The UN Charter and the Declaration on Independence favor national integrity and oppose secession or outside efforts to split a nation apart; but the definitions are not clear.

Moreover, the timing of self-determination for a particular people is a matter of dispute. In the 1963 debate over Portugal in the Security Council, the British view was that the main responsibility for deciding when a colonial people had been sufficiently prepared to choose sensibly whether to set up as an independent nation or to remain attached to the administering Power must lie with the administering Power itself. This position has much to be said for it if the Power is honestly trying to prepare the people for self-determination, which is not always the case. The general UN attitude has been one of watchful suspicion. The Charter specifies the UN right to supervise the administration of trust territories to make sure they are honestly being prepared for self-determination. The Assembly has gradually claimed the same right to supervise the treatment of all colonial territories.

The fact that a colonial people may be entirely incapable of sensible self-determination or self-government has been indicated by events such as those in the Congo, but it is flatly denied by two groups of UN members.

Most of the new states deny this fact for natural emotional reasons, since the pretext of unpreparedness has been used in cases where the people concerned felt it was unjustly applied. Hence the clause in the Declaration on Independence stating that lack of preparation shall never be used as a pretext for delaying independence. Fortunately this clause does not govern the administering Powers, or there would be more cases like the Congo.

The other group that rejects the fact of unpreparedness is the communist bloc. Disregarding its own refusal to allow self-determination to the East European countries, the Soviet Union joins in demanding immediate independence for all other colonies. Some of these are bases for defense against communist aggression. And any unprepared territory becoming prematurely independent is likely to fall into disorder, which may open the way for outside intervention and control.

With all these conflicting ideas and motives, the United Nations debates over colonialism and self-determination are bound to be distorted.

Like many other declarations by large assemblies, this Declaration uses extreme language that can be applied in real life only through interpretation that apparently contradicts some of the Declaration itself.

In the first place, the statement that lack of readiness shall not "serve as a pretext" for delaying independence does not apply to honest cases of delay while the people are being prepared, as was done for ten years under UN auspices in Somalia. No doubt there are some persons who, for good or bad motives, would like to see all sixty dependencies freed at once, regardless of chaos; but fortunately that is not likely to happen. One Congo or one Cyprus at a time is all the UN can afford. The Portuguese colonies will impose a heavy strain on UN resources if and when they are liberated, and it is fortunate that this did not occur at the same time as the Congo.

Another feature that requires interpretation is the statement that all "peoples" have the right of self-determination. This does not necessarily mean political independence as a sovereign nation. Some territories, if given the right to vote on their future, will choose to join another nation under some arrangement that offers a satisfactory kind of local self-government. Thus the two regions of the British Cameroons voted to join two neighboring nations; Puerto Rico is voluntarily under the United States flag as a self-governing commonwealth. Many of the former British and French colonies, on attaining independence, have chosen to maintain a close relation to the metropolitan Powers.

The work of the Special Committee, seeking to bring into effect the provisions of the Declaration, necessarily varies widely in different colonial areas because of varying circumstances. In April, 1964, for example, the Committee set up three subcommittees to examine a number of small island colonies. One would consider Mauritius, Seychelles, and St. Helena, all administered by Britain. Another would look at the Cook Islands, the Tokelau Islands, and Niue, administered by New Zealand; and American Samoa and Guam, administered by the United States, The third subcommittee was directed to consider the Virgin Islands, held by the United States, and the group of Caribbean islands controlled by Britain.

In the Committee discussion of these colonies, for example, the British spokesman described the growth of representative government in the island of Mauritius and stated that there was a general wish among the inhabitants to remain in the British Commonwealth after graduating into full independence. The representative of the neighboring country of Madagascar testified that his country was pleased to note that race relations on Mauritius were excellent, and that the people had a degree of self-government that could be the envy of many other African states.

New Zealand reported that the Cook Island group would become fully self-governing early in 1965, and that the Legislature, after full discussion, had decided on continuing association with New Zealand.

These are simple cases, chiefly marked by the fact that prosperity for the island people depends on trade with some advanced country, and their established business relations are with the administering Power.

A much more complicated situation is pictured in the Special Committee's long and largely fruitless debates on Aden and the Federation of South Arabia, where the United Kingdom has an important military base, and where it has been fighting with the tribes along the border of Yemen. According to the British claim, the Federation is progressing normally toward self-government, and the question of the military base will finally be settled by negotiations with a self-governing Federation. The disorders are attributed to subversion by agents from Yemen, backed by the United Arab Republic. The position of Yemen is that South Arabia is rightly a part of Yemen, illegally held by the British. The Soviet position is that all British military bases ought to be abolished whether the local inhabitants want them or not. The Asian and African states call it a "colonial war." The West European members say that the truth has not been made clear and that they have no proper basis for judging what ought to be done. The United States takes the same position.

No solution for this dispute seems possible in the near future.

The principle of self-determination is commonly taken to mean that every "people" has a right to decide by vote whether to be independent or to join with others as part of a larger sovereignty. In practice, however, the application of this principle depends on many complicated conditions.

At Versailles, after World War I, President Wilson tried to stand firmly for self-determination as the Peace Conference worked at redrawing the boundary lines of Europe. At some points he was frustrated by the demands of the victorious Allies who wanted territory for defense purposes or for other reasons not including the wishes of the inhabitants. At other points the principle of self-determination ran up against the fact that hostile peoples lived in the same territory. Some cruel mass migrations have been forced on the peoples of Europe to rearrange them into areas where they could be free of hostile fellow citizens. And there are still pockets of people who cannot govern themselves because they do not occupy the right land to make a workable nation.

Some of the difficulties in applying the principles of self-determination are illustrated by the experiences of the United States. Until the present century the United States was an expanding power, taking, buying, or conquering the western lands until it came to the Pacific, and at the same time taking in millions of immigrants from other countries, chiefly from Europe.

Then in the Spanish War of 1898 the United States captured Cuba, Puerto Rico, and the Philippines, and the reaction against imperialism set in. The people of the United States found that they did not want to govern foreign-speaking people in distant lands. They took measures to make these countries independent as soon as the inhabitants could successfully carry out the duties of independent nations.

On the other hand, the United States has made it

clear that no state in the Union can resign and set up for itself. This was settled in 1861–65 by one of the fiercest wars in history. The United States recognizes many Indian tribes as "nations" with treaty rights that include a considerable degree of self-government, subject, however, to veto by the United States Congress. But it does not allow immigrant groups to set up independent governments on its soil. They can vote in elections, and can vote as a German bloc or an Irish bloc if their leaders can hold the people together. But they cannot escape the sovereignty of the United States.

The UN has recognized such limitations on self-determination in the Declaration on Independence itself, where it condemns "any attempt aimed at the partial or total disruption of the national unity and the territorial integrity of a country." The UN opposition to the various secession movements in the Congo showed the same practical appreciation of the necessity of keeping the existing nations intact if possible, even though they may contain minorities that feel themselves unjustly treated.

These experiences have left the people of the United States strongly in favor of self-determination—but only where it is a practical way of living. They believe that any race or language group that wants to be an independent nation ought to be allowed to do so, provided it can be separated without serious trouble and can make a workable nation. Being a workable nation means coming close to paying its own expenses, helping its neighbors to keep the peace, and cooperating with the United Nations. By these standards not every small group of people that wants self-determination can get full national independence, or even self-government. But world opinion, as shown in the UN, is plainly favorable to the freedom of peoples wherever it is practicable.

— 7 —

INTERNATIONAL DISPUTES

One of the most important jobs of the United Nations is to settle international disputes if possible, or if they cannot be settled, to keep them under negotiation without shooting while time passes and passions may perhaps cool. Often the negotiations drag along for years with no final settlement. But as one UN delegate remarked, "It is better that old men get ulcers than that young men get shot."

It is sometimes said that in the world of the hydrogen bomb there is no alternative to the peaceful solution of disputes, since in an atomic war the only victor would be Death. This is true of a war between the Soviet Union and the United States, but it does not apply to the scores of countries that have no atomic bombs. They can fight with ordinary, or "conventional," weapons without losing more than a small percent of their populations. In Africa some tribes are still able to kill hundreds or thousands of their enemies with spears or arrows.

In actual practice, therefore, the UN has two quite different peace-keeping tasks. One is to use its influence to press the antagonists in the cold war to compromise their differences, to avoid "confrontations," or head-on collisions, and to get on with disarmament and the abolition of nuclear weapons. The other is to prevent or stop the old-fashioned wars that hotheaded people can carry on with no fear of total national suicide. There is all too much truth in the old belief that man is by nature a war-

115

like animal, though he is not often suicidal. Where people can fight without the fear of certain suicide, they are likely to do so.

Civilization has partially controlled the instinct for private murder, for family feuds, and for wars between adjoining cities. Between nations, disputes often are settled without killing. The United Nations is one more peacemaking institution, and it often succeeds in keeping or making peace, at least to the extent of stopping the guns. The two kinds of war and of peace-keeping are related by the fact that a small, or "brushfire," war may threaten to draw in the big Powers and grow into the fatal World War III. This is an added reason for rushing to put out any fire however small. For the present, most nations can see chances to fight without courting suicide, and many will choose to fight. In the long run, however, there is hope that the UN will be able to reduce the fighting below the level of 1964.

The following cases will serve to illustrate some of the UN peacemaking activities that have attracted widespread attention.

Syria-Lebanon

One of the earliest cases to come before the Security Council was the dispute over the failure of French and British troops to withdraw from Syria and Lebanon after the end of World War II. In February, 1946, Syria and Lebanon complained to the Council. The cause of the failure to withdraw was not any deep conflict between these countries and the British and French, but a failure of the British and French to agree between themselves on the conditions of evacuation. At the time there was danger that the dispute might be widely interpreted as the beginning of an unfortunate quarrel between two Western Powers over the exploitation of two weak countries of the Near East.

In the Security Council a resolution was proposed "expressing confidence" that the British and French would move out as soon as was practicable. This resolution was blocked by a Soviet veto, but its moral effect was not lessened by that. The British and French evacuated Syria in about two months and Lebanon a few months later.

Kashmir

When the British Government granted independence to India in 1947, it could not persuade the Hindus and Mohammedans to agree on setting up a single overall government. After much discussion the new nations of India and Pakistan were formed: one to contain a majority of Hindus and the other a majority of Moslems. A large and cruel exchange of populations took place, and there was severe rioting. Blood was hot.

By a part of the agreement the British rulers set free the mountain princedom of Jammu and Kashmir, with the right to decide for itself whether to join India or Pakistan. Shortly afterward there were reports of an invasion by Pakistani tribesmen. India complained to the Security Council on January 1, 1948. The situation was complicated by the fact that most of the population was Moslem, but the Prince, or Maharajah, was Hindu. The Maharajah had decided to join the state to India, and India had accepted.

India complained that Pakistan was guilty of aggression. Pakistan told the Security Council that it had tried without success to control the wild tribes on the border, and that the Maharajah's joining of India was illegal. Both sides were willing to let the people vote on the question once order had been restored.

The Security Council appointed a commission to investigate and mediate between the contending states.

The Council itself recommended that the two states should call home their people who were not regular residents of the territory, and that they should agree on a cease-fire. As soon as the disorders had quieted down, the Indian army should be reduced to the minimum needed for keeping order. Then there should be a free and impartial election to decide which nation would get the territory. The Council directed the commission to go to India and Pakistan and help to work out an agreement.

When the commission got to India in July, 1948, it learned that regular Pakistani troops were in Kashmir "to prevent a forcible seizure of the country by India." The situation looked more and more like war. The commission therefore proposed to both governments that they agree on a cease-fire and withdrawal of troops. It offered suggestions on how the voting was to be carried out. By December, India and Pakistan had agreed to a cease-fire as of January 1, 1949, with truce details to be decided later. The cease-fire line was settled the following July 27.

The commission then attacked the problem of getting the two sides to withdraw their forces so that peaceful conditions for voting could be established. It was unable to bring the parties to an agreement. In December, 1949, the commission reported a stalemate to the Council, and suggested that perhaps a single UN representative with broad powers might have better success.

General McNaughton of Canada, who was President of the Council in December, made an unsuccessful effort to bring about an agreement. In April the Council appointed Sir Owen Dixon of Australia as UN Representative, and his appointment was accepted by both India and Pakistan.

Sir Owen made a new effort to get a withdrawal of forces, but without success. He reported back to the Security Council and asked to be relieved.

The Council on April 30, 1951, appointed Dr. Frank Graham of the United States as UN Representative, and called upon the two governments to cooperate with him.

Dr. Graham talked with the governments of India and Pakistan during the summer of 1951. He found them willing to agree on proposals to avoid open warfare and warlike talk, and on the acceptance of the principle of deciding the issue by a vote. But they could not agree about how and when to demilitarize.

Dr. Graham reported the situation to the Council, which directed him to continue his efforts. The Soviet delegate objected, saying that the UN efforts had been really intended to support a British and American plot to get a military base in Kashmir. He suggested leaving the whole matter to the people of Kashmir.

From then on, as the years passed, both sides reduced their armed forces in the territory, but no agreement on a vote of the people was reached. In February, 1957, the Security Council sent Gunnar Jarring of Sweden to see if any settlement could be agreed upon. He found the leaders of both countries ready to talk with "complete frankness and cordiality," but with no signs of agreeing.

Mr. Jarring reported that he had no proposals for a settlement but that both India and Pakistan seemed to want to find a solution.

The UN position all along was that the two parties should hasten to reduce their armed forces in Kashmir and make arrangements for a vote. This UN request has made slow headway. But in the meantime, the shooting was stopped; India and Pakistan continued to sit side by side in specialized agency committees and other UN activities, often voting together. By 1954 the two governments had established direct conferences between their prime ministers, and the danger of war appeared to be over. From 1957 to 1960 the Security Council had no discussion of this conflict, though it received a number of communications from the governments involved.

In 1962, when India had to appeal to Britain and the United States for aid against an attack by Communist China, both countries put pressure on India to settle with Pakistan, so as to free the Indian troops stationed in Kashmir for service on the Chinese border. But before a settlement was reached the attack ceased, and the Kashmir operation remained unresolved.

In December, 1963, violent religious feelings flared among the Moslems in Kashmir over the disappearance of a venerated relic, the hair of Mohammed, from a shrine in Srinagar. The Indian Government hastily sent investigators to look into the matter. The holy relic was restored and the sense of outrage grew less acute, but the situation remained farther than ever from a peaceful solution. At the other end of the country, where since 1962 India had been gradually expelling Moslems into East Pakistan, riots broke out against the Hindu minority, and thousands of them fled into Eastern India, carrying the seeds of religious hatred with them. In the spring of 1964 mobs in Calcutta and other Indian towns were killing Moslems. Those Moslems who could, fled to East Pakistan. The Government of Pakistan appealed to the Security Council, accusing India of amalgamating Kashmir into its political system, and thus disregarding the previous decision of the

Council that the people ought to be allowed to vote on which country they preferred. To this accusation India replied that Kashmir was undoubtedly a part of India and that the people could not be permitted to vote themselves out. Meanwhile Chou En-lai, of Communist China, visiting Pakistan, spoke in favor of a Pakistani "war of liberation" in Kashmir. The situation in 1964 remained ominous, but it could at least be claimed that UN influence had, so far, restrained open warfare between Pakistan and India—warfare that would have opened both countries to conquest from the north.

In February, 1964, however, a meeting was arranged between the home ministers of India and Pakistan. At this meeting agreements were reached that considerably eased the religious conflicts. Another favorable event was the release of Sheik Abdullah, the revered Kashmiri leader, who had been held in jail since 1958 on charges of conspiring with Pakistan.

The members of the Security Council, debating the situation in May, 1964, expressed satisfaction at these developments and urged the two countries to continue direct negotiations.

The Berlin Blockade

In September, 1948, France, the United Kingdom, and the United States complained to the Security Council that the Soviet Union had cut off land communications between the Western zones of Germany and Berlin. The Council voted to discuss the blockade as a threat to the peace—over the protest of the U.S.S.R., which contended that the measures had been necessitated by currency reforms in the Western zones that threatened the Soviet zone with economic collapse. Various members of the Council tried to find a solution that both sides would accept, but the proposed draft was vetoed by the Soviets. The President of the Assembly and the Secretary-General, basing themselves on an Assembly appeal to the Great Powers to "compose their differences and establish a lasting peace," also urged the parties to hunt for a means of agreement, but with no immediate result.

In the meantime, the Western Powers supplied Berlin

by air, with spectacular success, and informal talks among the UN representatives of the four occupying Powers soon led to an agreement. It was universally recognized in this case that a reasonable solution of the trouble would have been much harder to arrange if the opposing parties had not been able to meet easily and informally in the corridors of the UN building.

This solution held for a dozen years but was increasingly painful to the Soviet Union, since Berlin served as an escape hatch for thousands of East Germans. Communist demands for a change rose to a crisis in 1960 and 1961, and the possible influence of the UN toward finding a peaceful solution was not readily apparent.

In 1961, the Soviet Union built a wall across Berlin in an effort to stop the flood of refugees escaping to the West, and the dispute over Berlin seemed to be growing more acute. But further developments in the "cold war" between the communist and noncommunist blocs appeared in 1963 to have reduced the tension at this point.

During the Christmas season of 1963, the Wall was temporarily opened so that West Berliners might cross into East Berlin to visit their relatives living there. The communists took severe precautions to prevent the escape of East Berliners during this truce. An effort was made at Easter time in 1964 to repeat this visiting period, but without success.

Palestine

The United Nations inherited the situation in Palestine. That territory had been placed under a British mandate by the League of Nations. In 1947 the British Government asked the UN Assembly to look into the Palestine question. The Assembly decided that Palestine should be divided between Jewish and Arab states, except for Jerusalem, which would have an international government. The plan provided that the British mandate should end by August 1, 1948. But it soon became evident that there was going to be trouble between the Jews and the Arabs. The Assembly on May 20 appointed Count Folke Bernadotte, President of the Swedish Red Cross, as Mediator.

The British gave up their mandate on May 15, and the

new state of Israel was proclaimed. Soon the Arab states were marching against Israel. The Council called on all governments to abstain from war in Palestine. It issued a cease-fire order on May 22. By June 9 the Mediator had received the agreement of all parties to a truce, starting June 11, to last four weeks.

At the end of the four weeks the Arab states refused to extend the truce, and fighting broke out again. On September 17, 1948, Count Folke Bernadotte and the chief of the French observers, Colonel André Sérot, were assassinated in the Jewish sector of Jerusalem. Dr. Ralph Bunche of the United States, who was acting as assistant to the Mediator, was directed to take over.

During the last three months of 1948 there were several outbreaks of fighting, but the truce was restored on January 7, 1949, with troop withdrawal and supervision by UN observers. During the next six months all the Arab states signed armistice agreements with Israel. The Security Council urged the states to negotiate a final peace settlement. Dr. Bunche was awarded the Nobel Peace Prize for his work in Palestine.

The Assembly, on December 9, 1949, directed the Trusteeship Council to administer the international City of Jerusalem, but both Arabs and Jews refused to give up their parts of the city. The Jews even moved in some departments of their government.

After 1949 the relations between Jews and Arabs failed to improve. The UN Truce Supervision Organization reported many violations and disputes. A particularly dangerous dispute arose over the refusal of Egypt to let ships bound for Israel pass through the Suez Canal. Repeated efforts of the Security Council failed to persuade Egypt to lift these restrictions, and the situation remained tense. All the Arab states made it plain that they would never reconcile themselves to the existence of Israel.

Suez

In the summer of 1956 Egypt received large shipments of arms from Czechoslovakia which were stacked in the Sinai Desert, near to the Israeli border. Israel accused Egypt of planning war, and also complained of increasing raids by Egyptian bands known as *fedayeen*. The United States withdrew a previous offer of a loan to Egypt for building the Aswan Dam on the Nile, saying that excessive purchase of communist arms had undermined Egypt's ability to pay. Egypt reacted by seizing control of the Suez Canal on July 26, 1956.

The Suez Canal had been dug, through Egyptian territory, under a concession negotiated in 1888, and was owned and operated by a corporation, the Universal Suez Canal Company, the stock of which was held largely in England and France. Egypt offered to pay for the stock at the prices of the day before the seizure, but that did not satisfy the users. Led by Britain, France, and the United States, they tried to negotiate an acceptable agreement with Egypt, but without success, and on September 12, France and Britain complained to the Security Council. Negotiations were still under way when on October 29 the United States informed the Council that Israel had invaded Egypt in violation of the armistice. The United States called for an immediate meeting.

Israel charged that Egypt was building up its system of *fedayeen* raids not merely to harass but to destroy Israel, and that self-defense had made it necessary to seize the *fedayeen* bases.

On October 30, Britain and France called on Egypt and Israel to stop fighting and withdraw their forces ten miles from the Canal so as to avoid blocking traffic. They asked Egypt to agree to let them temporarily occupy the canal zone, which Egypt refused. In the Security Council the United States offered a resolution calling for a cease-fire and calling upon all members not to use force in the area. This was vetoed by Britain and France, and their aircraft began bombing military targets in Egypt the next day. The Security Council then called the Assembly into emergency session.

The Assembly met November 1 and urged that all parties agree to a cease-fire. The British and French, insisting on the necessity for police action, were willing to withdraw only if Egypt and Israel would consent to the sending of a United Nations force to keep the peace. On November 5 the Assembly voted to establish such a force, and it was assembled with great speed in the next few

days. Ten nations, none of them being among the Great
Powers, provided the troops. Much of the transport and
supplies were contributed by Italy, where the force was
assembled, and by Sweden and the United States. The
first unit of the UN Emergency Force was flown into
Egypt on November 15.

At the time of the cease-fire, Israel had captured most
of the Sinai Peninsula, together with great stores of arms,
and the Anglo-French forces had occupied the northern
end of the Canal. As these forces withdrew the UNEF
advanced, acting as a buffer to prevent contact between
them and the Egyptians, until the UNEF came to rest
along the Israeli border, where it settled down to the job
of patrolling and preventing raids. It also took over from
Israeli forces the forts on the narrow neck of the Gulf of
Aqaba, which the Egyptians had previously used to block
access to the Israeli port of Eilat, Israel's only door to the
Far East.

The ships that had been sunk in the Canal were removed
by contractors from Denmark and the Netherlands, with
aid from other nations not involved in the conflict, working
under UN auspices. The Canal was clear by the middle of
April, 1957, and was opened for traffic under the Suez
Canal Authority, which Egypt had created in July, 1956.

The net results of the flare-up in Egypt did not settle
the conflicts between Israel and the Arab states or between
Egypt and the users of the Suez Canal. Conditions in the
Middle East remained highly explosive. But for the moment the influence of the United Nations, and the threat
of Soviet intervention, had succeeded in quenching an outbreak that might have led to a much bigger war.

A by-product of the UN action was the invention of a
new kind of police force, the UNEF. The Assembly made
it clear that this force was not intended to take any part
against one side or the other, but only to prevent "in-
cidents" and renewed fighting. The questions in dispute
must be left for negotiation, however long that might take.
The central principle is that in the present explosive state
of the world no actual shooting is allowable. Military
power still has a large place in the negotiations of nations,
but its use as a "deterrent" is accepted only as an unfortunate and dangerous necessity, to be mitigated if

possible by disarmament. Meanwhile the UN does not recognize that any injustice or threat could justify starting a shooting war.

The UNEF was armed enough to stop a riot but not enough to resist an attack by an organized military force. Its defense was moral. Any of the four contending nations that would attack a unit of the UNEF would be shooting the "soldiers of peace," as they were called. These were men from Brazil or Finland, India or Yugoslavia, who had come there to stand together in the line of fire so that no one could shoot at an enemy without killing a friend. As it worked out, even the civilian population treated the UNEF soldiers as friends. There were few signs of riot, and they soon disappeared. The moral protection worked.

In fact, UNEF has proved so useful along the Israeli-Arab border that it is hard to see when it can be withdrawn. In 1959 the Secretary-General reported to the General Assembly that conditions remained generally quiet, but if it were to be brought home there might be dangerous outbreaks. The force had been cut down as far as was safe, but it seemed to be a long-term enterprise that would require some more dependable method of financing than "assessments" that too often were not being promptly paid.

The UNEF is surely not all the world needs for keeping the peace, especially as such a force cannot even enter a fighting zone unless the belligerents first agree to a cease-fire. And there are still underlying conflicts of nations that must either be settled or lived down through the passage of time, if war is to be avoided. But every example of peacemaking is one step toward a more peaceful world. The UNEF was an invention that might find uses in future areas of tension.

Arab Refugees

In November, 1948, the General Assembly authorized a loan of $5,000,000 for the immediate relief of the Arabs who had fled from Israel, and urged the nations to make up a fund of $32,000,000 for the next ten months. The United Nations Relief for Palestine Refugees (UNRPR) was established, and received contributions of $35,000,000 from thirty-three governments. There were about 900,000 refugees to be cared for at that time.

A year later the Assembly decided to try a program of work relief—road building, forest planting, and other enterprises—that might open up new industries in which the refugees could become self-supporting. A Relief and Works Agency (UNRWA) was created, with Henry R. Labouisse of the U.S.A. as Director.

Some little progress was made in the first ten years. By 1959, although there were now over a million refugees registered with UNRWA, many thousands not registered or drawing assistance from that organization were living and working in various parts of the Arab world. About 40 percent of the refugees were living in camps built mainly with refugee labor. UNRWA was able to report that the vocational training programs and the loans for workers to set up small enterprises of their own were both "highly successful and are accepted by the refugees and the local governments," but funds were too limited and there were long waiting lists, a cruel example of having to save at the spigot and waste at the bung. UNRWA is assisted in its work by more than thirty international or foreign voluntary organizations and—an encouraging point—by a large number of small local groups in the host countries.

A proposal for a Jordan Valley Authority was put forward by Dr. Walter Lowdermilk of the U.S. Soil Conservation Service after World War II. The development of the Jordan River would supply water to irrigate much of the land in the district that is suitable for farming, and would provide jobs for hundreds of thousands of the refugees in the Arab parts of the valley. The benefits to be had by all concerned from loyally working together on this project would offer good reasons for keeping the peace. A successful Jordan Valley Authority, if established, might well stand as a good example of a practical instrument that might be used in other places where national interests overlap a territory that is rich in possibilities for united development.

Czechoslovakia

In March, 1948, after the communist revolution in Czechoslovakia, the Security Council considered a complaint by Dr. Jan Papanek, permanent UN representative from the old Czechoslovak Government. Dr. Papanek accused the U.S.S.R. of violating the independence of Czechoslovakia by a threat of force, and charged that the Soviets had helped directly and indirectly in the overthrow of his government.

The Soviet delegate denied the charges and said they had been brought up for the purpose of poisoning international relations and striking a blow at the United Nations. The new Government of Czechoslovakia refused to take part in the discussion, saying it was an interference in the country's internal affairs and contrary to the Charter.

Proposals to instruct a committee to look into the evidence were blocked by a Soviet veto. No results of any kind could be had in this case, and the Council, in the legal language of the report, "remained seized of the question."

Korea

The Korean outbreak was unique in several ways. The Republic of Korea had been endorsed by the UN, since the Assembly on December 12, 1948, declared that a lawful government had been established in South Korea. When, therefore, the North Korean forces crossed the 38th parallel on June 25, 1950, and invaded the Republic of Korea, the attack struck directly at the United Nations. If this attack had succeeded, the UN could be expected to fall apart as the League of Nations had done after it failed to act when the Japanese took Manchuria, Mussolini took Ethiopia, and Hitler took Czechoslovakia.

The second unique feature was the fact that the Soviet Union was boycotting the Security Council because it refused to give the Chinese seat to a delegate from Communist China. The Council was therefore able to act, in the absence of a Soviet veto, and it called into being a United Nations army to resist the invasion. This kind of resistance to aggression could of course never happen again, but it happened on this occasion and undoubtedly saved the United Nations from extinction.

As a result of the resistance of the ROK army and its UN allies, the invasion was eventually thrown back to the 38th parallel, where it started, and a truce was established.

Uniting for Peace

When the Assembly met in September, 1950, the need for some better arrangements to deal with future aggressions was plain. The original plan, adopted in 1945, was evidently not practicable under the conditions that had developed since that time.

The Charter originally provided for a UN police force, which many people hoped might in time grow to be stronger than any national military power. The police force was to be placed under the control of the Security Council, on which sat the Great Powers with their right of veto. It had to be assumed that all the Great Powers would stand against aggression, otherwise the UN system for enforcing peace by police power would of course break down. The idea of a world police force recalls the plan urged during World War I by William Howard Taft and other prominent citizens for a League to Enforce Peace—a forerunner of Mr. Wilson's proposal of the League of Nations.

Although the Security Council had never been able to agree on the organization of the UN police, it found itself in Korea possessed of a fighting force contributed by sixteen member nations. The command was delegated to the United States by action of the Council, and the Council symbolized its authority by raising the UN flag over the UN armies. Thus for once there was a UN force enforcing peace. But it could not happen again in any case where the Great Powers were not unanimous in their support. Something different would have to be tried.

The United States, therefore, brought into the General Assembly a set of resolutions called "Uniting for Peace." This proposal was discussed at length and finally passed on November 3, 1950, by 52 votes to 5, with 2 members abstaining. The 5 votes in opposition were those of the Soviet Union, Byelorussia, Czechoslovakia, Poland, and the Ukraine.

Under the new rule, if any sudden aggression breaks out, the Assembly can be called into emergency session on twenty-four hours' notice by any seven members of the Security Council in case the Council is blocked by a veto. Once the Assembly is in session, it can pass a resolution advising the member states of the emergency and calling upon them to help the victim by military and other means.

The adoption of the Uniting for Peace resolutions came only after a long and serious debate, in which the very nature of the United Nations was examined. The Soviet delegate, opposing the resolutions, said that they were designed to weaken the Security Council by taking away its full responsibility for peace and security. The Soviet argument pointed out that the "principle of unanimity," that is, the veto, would be evaded if the Assembly could act when the Council was stopped by a veto.

The spokesmen for the resolutions said that under the Charter the Assembly had always had the right to express its opinion on any matter not being handled by the Council. In other words, the majority in the Assembly, by passing these resolutions, was asserting that the veto could block action only in the Council, but in so doing would leave the question free for consideration in the Assembly.

It should be said that the veto power was originally attached to the police power that was intended to be at the disposal of the Security Council. The United States insisted that if the UN was to have a police force it must be controlled by a body in which the United States could not be outvoted. All the other Great Powers felt the same way, since it was plainly impossible to have a peace organization attempting to discipline a Great Power by military force. The Uniting for Peace resolutions were not designed with any ideas that the Assembly would organize a war against a first-class Power, i.e., would start World War III. They were designed to provide for suppression of a small or brushfire war in which no Great Power is prepared to fight openly on the side of the aggressor. That is what was done in Korea, but it was only an accident that the Security Council was able to act. Now the Assembly can act.

If any new war should flare up between small states or

parties in a state, it may well be that the aggressor is secretly backed by one of the Great Powers, but that the backer, while prepared to veto any Security Council action, is not prepared to fight openly at the risk of a world war. In such a case the Assembly could promptly declare which side is the aggressor, and other Great Powers could then come in on the side of the victim, as several did in Korea, without necessarily starting World War III. It seems possible that since 1950 a number of brushfire wars in various parts of the world may have been prevented by this new ability of the Assembly to give an authoritative sanction to aid for the victim.

The flexibility of the UN is illustrated by the different uses that have actually been made of the Uniting for Peace machinery. In the Suez crisis, the Assembly could not, of course, think of raising a force to fight against the two Great Powers that were engaged. But it met in emergency session, found that all the belligerents were willing to call off the fighting, and created an entirely new type of military force to police the armistice. In the Hungarian crisis no military operation under UN auspices was feasible, but the Assembly was able to take a political action against the aggressor that would have been impossible in the Security Council.

Whether future crises can be successfully handled is of course impossible to say. But in Korea the United Nations not only escaped a mortal danger but also strengthened its constitution against future dangers.

The Congo

The UNEF experience in Palestine served as a valuable guide in mid-1960 when the Republic of the Congo attained independence on June 30. For the most part, the Congolese were without education or any technical and administrative experience. The result, complicated by the military situation, was chaos.

The Congo is one of the richest underdeveloped areas in the world. In the nineteenth century, a collapse of this kind would have brought in the European colonial Powers to restore order, divide up the territory, and establish colonial administrations. But the world of 1960 could not endure any such intervention, especially since the Soviet Union and the United States would inevitably have been involved.

As Walter Lippmann, the great political commentator, observed, no practical cure for this dangerous crisis could be imagined without the United Nations, which "would have to be invented if it did not already exist." Even that would have offered poor prospects of success, in comparison with the use of the present going concern with its fifteen years of stormy experience back of it.

In Walter Lippmann's words: "This UN enterprise is the most advanced and the most sophisticated experiment in international cooperation ever attempted. Among all that is so sad and so mean and so sour in world politics, it is heartening to think that something so good and so pure in its purpose is possible. No one can say that the experiment will succeed. But there is no doubt that it deserves to succeed."

The Congo situation was also rendered dangerous by the presence of technical advisers from Belgium and from the Soviet Union, with corresponding partisans among the Congolese political leaders. The Soviet technicians were soon sent home, but their partisans remained active. The Belgians held on in spite of UN demands for their withdrawal, and under Belgian influence the richest province, Katanga, seceded and set itself up as a separate nation.

The Soviet Union became violently opposed to the UN operation and demanded that the UN force be withdrawn, and that the office of Secretary-General be replaced with a three-man board, or "troika," on which the U.S.S.R. would have a veto. There was much disorder in the Congo during the winter of 1960–61, and in February Patrice Lumumba, a leader favored by the Soviets, was murdered.

The expressed purposes of the UN operation in the Congo were to help the Government maintain law and order, to prevent civil war and tribal conflicts, and to maintain the territorial integrity of the nation. The operation was also designed to protect the country from outside interference, particularly by foreign mercenary soldiers of fortune. Finally, it was to help in the restoration of industry and the public services, training Congolese to take over work formerly done by the departing Europeans.

The UN military force was authorized to shoot only in self-defense, for the prevention of civil war, and for the expulsion of mercenaries. The mercenaries were soldiers of fortune hired at high pay out of the profits of the rich Katangan mines. They numbered between 500 and 600 men, mainly Belgian and French, and served as officers in the Katangan army. They not only protected the President of Katanga, Moise Tshombe, against revolting tribesmen, but also fought the UN troops.

The UN made repeated efforts to negotiate with Mr. Tshombe; at times he renounced his attempted secession, at other times he encouraged the mercenaries to resist and to obstruct free movements of UN forces in the province. It was on a trip to meet Mr. Tshombe that the Secretary-General of the UN, Dag Hammarskjöld, lost his life in an airplane crash. To succeed him U Thant of Burma was chosen Acting Secretary-General.

In August, 1962, Mr. Thant presented a National Reconciliation Plan, which was accepted by the central government and by Mr. Tshombe. The Plan proposed a federal system; a sharing of the export revenues, earned mainly by the Katanga mines; and the incorporation of all military forces such as those of Katanga in the National Army.

In December, 1962, since Mr. Tshombe had taken no effective action to fulfill his part in the agreement, the UN forces advanced in Southern Katanga, mopping up or driving out the mercenaries; and by January, 1963, the secession movement seemed to be at an end. In this advance there were some casualties, but they were relatively few because of the good discipline and restraint of the UN soldiers.

After the country was cleared of mercenaries there remained the slow job of reconstruction and development, carried out through the cooperation of the UN and its specialized agencies, aided by the return of some of the Belgian technicians and businessmen who had fled in 1960 at the start of the troubles. By 1963 the situation appeared to have improved so far as to remove the danger to world peace that had loomed so darkly in 1960. There were tribal outbursts in which several missionaries were murdered; but in general, peace began to prevail. The cost, to the end of 1962, had been nearly 300 million dollars, a small amount compared with the costs of war. It almost bankrupted the UN, however, because of the refusal of some members, led by the U.S.S.R. and France, to pay their assessments. But precarious though the Congo operation was, it did save the world from a dangerous confrontation of the Soviet Union and the United States.

By March, 1964, conditions in the Congo were visibly better. The central government had a balanced budget, and was beginning to contribute substantially to the UN expenses, which were rapidly tapering off with the reduction of UN military forces. Prices were stabilized. The Belgian Foreign Minister, Paul Henri Spaak, visited the Congo and negotiated a settlement under which Belgium turned over to the Congolese Government some 750 million dollars worth of industrial shares, and also relieved it of a debt of about 500 million dollars. In return, the Belgians would be allowed to restore business relations that would be profitable both to them and to the Congolese.

During this period, while the disorders in the Congo made the news that attracted world attention, the civilian services of the UN and its family of agencies were quietly building the foundations on which the hope of future peace and prosperity must rest. This has been the largest program of technical assistance in any one nation in the history of the UN. Whereas in other developing countries technical assistance offers a chance to hasten the improvement of living standards, in the Congo a massive program was necessary to prevent total collapse and chaos.

The civilian experts and technicians from various UN agencies numbered about 600 at any given time. They dealt with all aspects of life in a modern nation for which no sufficient number of Congolese had been trained before the country became independent: transport, health, education, civil aviation, public works, mining, weather reporting, improvement of agriculture, as well as public administration and national economics. In a word they very nearly had to build a civilization from the ground up. Meanwhile the Congolese Government was struggling to establish control of the country.

When the last of the UN military forces left the country

at the end of June, 1964, the political situation was still insecure. There were savage tribal revolts in some of the eastern provinces, stirred up by Chinese Communist agents who preached racial war against all Europeans. Mr. Tshombe, who had gone to Europe after the end of the Katanga secession, returned to Léopoldville, and was chosen to lead a coalition government.

The UN civilian advisers remained as the best hope for a successful outcome, but it was clearly unfortunate that the UN could not afford the expense of continued military assistance.

Malaysia

In 1963, when the former British colonies of Malaya, Singapore, North Borneo, and Sarawak planned to unite, forming the new state of Malaysia (with the consent and encouragement of Britain), objections were heard from Indonesia and the Philippines. Both these countries claimed territorial rights in Borneo that conflicted with the British colonial power in North Borneo and Sarawak.

The governments of Malaya, Indonesia, and the Philippines joined in asking the UN to find out and report whether the people of Sarawak and North Borneo wanted to join with Malaya and Singapore in the proposed federation. They said they would willingly abide by the Secretary-General's conclusion in the matter. No plebiscite was held, but there had recently been a parliamentary election, won by the candidates favorable to the federation.

In response, the Secretary-General appointed a mission composed of members of the UN Secretariat, which left immediately for Borneo. One team was to survey opinion in North Borneo, the other in Sarawak. The principles for judging whether the people had been given an honest chance for self-determination—on the basis of which a country could decide to join freely with another country into a single sovereign state—were those established by the General Assembly in 1960.

According to these principles the country must already have a high degree of self-government so that the people can make decisions by democratic processes—universal adult suffrage, full knowledge of the issues, and no intimidation.

The teams interviewed political and business leaders, tribal chiefs and village headmen, representatives of all sorts of organizations, and even political prisoners who had not been allowed to vote. They reported that the few hundred political prisoners came from districts that, as a rule, had voted against the federation and that the vote would not have been affected in any substantial way if the prisoners had been freed. The teams found no evidence that the outcome of the elections had been determined by fraud or intimidation, and they found that the leaders of the party opposed to federation agreed with this conclusion.

The Secretary-General therefore concluded that sizable majorities of the people in both Sarawak and North Borneo were in favor of joining the Federation of Malaysia.

Despite this authoritative judgment by U Thant, the Secretary-General, himself a native of Burma in Southeast Asia, peace was not restored. President Sukarno, of Indonesia, the expansionist tendencies of which country had already been demonstrated in the case of western New Guinea (West Irian), refused to accept the findings. He declared that Malaysia was still a British colony and that he would destroy it. He launched extensive guerrilla attacks in the jungles of Borneo. In January, 1964, Mr. Robert Kennedy, representing President Johnson of the United States, visited the area and persuaded Mr. Sukarno to accept a cease-fire and a conference, but there were signs that the conflict was far from over.

The International Court *of Justice, a World Court*

The International Court of Justice was established by a Statute which was made a part of the Charter. All members of the UN are "parties to the Statute," with voting rights in the choice of judges; and nonmembers can be admitted to the Statute on conditions laid down by the Security Council and the General Assembly.

Only states may be parties in cases before the Court,

over

and only if they agree to submit to the Court's decision. Members can take their disputes before boards of arbitration or other tribunals of their own choice; but if they come into the Court they are bound to accept the Court's judgment.

A state may also declare that it promises in general to submit any and all questions of certain kinds to the Court, if an opposing state also agrees to the Court's jurisdiction. By 1963, thirty-seven states had accepted compulsory jurisdiction. The standard agreement covers all disputes about the interpretation of treaties, the application of international law, the existence of any fact that would be a breach of an obligation, and the amount of damages payable for the breach.

The Court is the successor to the Permanent Court of International Justice at The Hague. It is authorized to take jurisdiction in cases under old treaties that provided for the settlement of disputes by the former Court. The Court not only settles disputes between nations, but gives advisory opinions to the UN and its agencies on matters of international law or interpretation of the Charter.

The Court is made up of fifteen judges, no two from the same nation. They are elected as persons, not as representatives of their nations, by the Security Council and the Assembly voting separately without any veto.

If the Court does not include any judge of the nationality of a state that is a party to a pending case, that state is entitled to choose a person to sit as a judge for that case. This is contrary to the usual judicial principle by which a judge disqualifies himself from sitting in any case where he has a personal interest; it represents here a relic of the tradition of arbitration rather than judicial decision.

The Court has already decided a number of cases where the parties were in disagreement about the meaning of treaties or of international law.

One of the first cases to come before the Court was the Corfu Channel case, in which the United Kingdom complained that Albania had laid mines in the channel without due notice, because of which British warships passing through were severely damaged, and some crew members were killed. Albania, in turn, accused the British of violating her territorial waters. The Court decided that the British had committed no wrong by peacefully passing through the Corfu Straits, and that Albania was responsible for the fact that the channel was mined, whether she laid the mines or allowed others to do so. The Court ruled that Albania should pay £844,000 as damages. It also found that the British, by coming later into the straits and sweeping mines without Albania's permission, had violated Albanian sovereignty, but need pay no damages on that account.

In 1959 Cambodia complained to the Court that Thailand had occupied a plot of Cambodian borderland containing the ruins of a holy monastery, a sacred place of pilgrimage. The dispute was settled by a finding of the Court that the territory belonged to Cambodia. The Court ordered Thailand to withdraw its soldiers or police and restore any sculptures that it had removed.

One of the most important advisory opinions of the Court was delivered in July, 1950, at the request of the General Assembly, on the status of South West Africa. The Court declared that although the League of Nations was dead, the League mandate under which South Africa governed the territory was not dead but had been inherited by the United Nations, to which South Africa was under obligation to report.

Another most important decision of the Court, given in July, 1962, ruled that the cost of the peace-keeping operations in the Congo was a UN expense subject to the Charter provisions for assessment by the Assembly, and that failure to pay the assessments could therefore be subject to the penalties provided in the Charter.

In April, 1957, as a sequel to its seizure of the Suez Canal, the Egyptian Government deposited with the UN a declaration stating how it proposed to operate the Canal. It pledged itself to abide by the Convention of 1888 that established the international character of the Canal. In a later declaration, on July 18, Egypt formally accepted as compulsory the jurisdiction of the Court in all legal disputes that might arise over the interpretation of the Convention or other treaty provisions relating to the Canal.

International Law Commission

The General Assembly in 1947 created the International Law Commission to write a code of international law. The Commission started with a draft of a Declaration of the Rights and Duties of States. Rights include the right to political independence, to govern the state's territory, and to fight in self-defense. Duties include keeping treaty promises, settling all disputes by peaceful means, refraining from using force without UN authorization, and respecting the basic rights of all citizens and aliens in the state's jurisdiction. At its 1949 session the Assembly recommended the draft to the attention of member states and asked for comments and advice.

The Commission was particularly asked to draft the principles of international law covering war crimes, as developed in the trials of Nazi war criminals at Nürnberg. It has also studied the principle of reservations which may be made by a nation at the time of ratifying an international agreement. The Commission suggested that future conventions should contain a provision making clear what would be the position in case of ratification with reservations.

Other questions studied by the Commission have included the possibility of defining aggression and of defining offenses against the peace and security of mankind. There is much difference of opinion among member states, not only as to exactly what acts would surely amount to aggression, but also as to whether it is safe to make a list of such acts. Some members fear that an aggressor, if provided with an exact list, would find ways of attack not positively included in the list, and so create confusion at the moment when the world should be uniting to resist what everyone knows to be an attack.

The Commission has prepared a draft of a code of arbitration procedures, and another for the international laws of nationality and statelessness. It has made studies of the possibility of setting up an International Criminal Court, to try people accused of international crimes such as genocide.

The 1956 session of the Commission was devoted mainly to a codification of the law of the sea. The Commission recommended a general international conference, at which many points not yet settled might be put in the way of international agreement. The General Assembly voted in February, 1957, to call such a conference for early in 1958. The program of the conference included such questions as the limits of the territorial sea, the right of innocent passage, fishing and oil-drilling rights on the continental shelf, the nationality of ships, penal jurisdiction in cases of collision, sea pollution, the slave trade, and piracy, including piracy by aircraft.

By developing international law, by settling some kinds of disputes in court, and by direct action in the Security Council or the Assembly to urge the nations to keep the peace, the UN has a long list of successes to its credit. Some disputes have been settled so completely that none of the parties concerned has any intention of bringing them up again. Some have merely been quelled, leaving both sides still enemies but not in a state of all-out war. Some of the disputes were of little consequence, since the parties were not likely to fight over the matter anyway, yet their settlement added to the orderly process of world association. Some disputes were important, because if they had flared up into heavy fighting the structure of world peace could have been dangerously undermined.

In all cases, settlements and judicial decisions help to build the framework for a peaceful world. Principles once established and then used in the decision of still other disputes gain respect. They stand as obstacles to future quarrels, cooling the blood of angry patriots who in the first flush of excitement may think they have more right on their side than later judgment will allow. All this work of conciliation, settlement, and definition, some of it too prosaic to make the front pages of the newspapers, is quietly building foundations upon which, if there is time, a solid world peace may someday be erected.

— 8 —

REGIONAL ARRANGEMENTS

According to the UN Charter, member nations may form regional alliances to maintain peace and security, provided these activities are "consistent with the Purposes and Principles of the United Nations." In 1945, when the Charter was adopted, the main purpose of this clause was to avoid disturbing the rapidly growing organization of the American republics, which had already come to be a force for peace and understanding in the Western Hemisphere. It was generally expected, however, that future disagreements among the UN members could be settled within the United Nations, and that there would not be much practical need for regional defense alliances. This expectation turned out to be premature.

Military alliances have grown up among the North Atlantic countries and the Western Pacific countries, in addition to agreements for strengthening the collective security of the American republics. Economic and political arrangements have also come into being in Western Europe looking toward some kind of federal European union. All these alliances and united agencies are designed to fortify the peace by military, economic, and political cooperation. They are auxiliaries to the United Nations. They cover areas smaller than the UN worldwide field of action —regions in which the nations have in common more principles and traditions of united action than are to be found in the broader society of the world as a whole.

140

NATO

The Western European and North American allies de-mobilized their armed forces as rapidly as possible after World War II. Their people did not expect any further trouble that would call for large-scale military defense, and they wanted the boys home.

Later these nations became convinced that the Soviet Union had not demobilized on anything like the same scale. Five of the countries of Western Europe, therefore, decided to unite and build up their defense forces. Britain, France, Belgium, the Netherlands, and Luxembourg signed a Western Union defense treaty in Brussels on March 17, 1948. As soon as the news of this treaty reached Washington, President Truman welcomed the action and declared that the United States would be glad to help.

The United States Senate adopted on June 11 a resolution recommending that the United States join in regional arrangements for collective security. With this backing, the President began negotiations with other countries in the North Atlantic area. These negotiations led to the North Atlantic Treaty, which was signed on April 12, 1949.

The twelve original members of the North Atlantic Treaty Organization, or NATO, were Belgium, Canada, Denmark, France, Iceland, Italy, Luxembourg, the Netherlands, Norway, Portugal, the United Kingdom, and the United States. Greece and Turkey joined in Feburary, 1952.

The principal section of the Treaty is Article 5, in which the members pledge themselves to consider an attack on any one of them as an attack on all. Article 3 pledges the members to cooperate in increasing their defensive strength by self-help and mutual aid. In Article 2, the members promise to build up their free institutions and to avoid economic conflicts among themselves. The treaty provides in Article 7 that it shall not be so interpreted as to affect in any way the obligations of the members to the United Nations, and it recognizes "the primary responsibility of the Security Council for the maintenance of international peace and security." In case of sudden attack the NATO forces will act as may be necessary and will immediately report to the Security Council. If the Security

Council is able to take the necessary measures, NATO will withdraw and leave the Security Council in sole charge.

In September, 1950, as part of the new thinking that resulted from the attack in Korea, the Council of NATO unanimously agreed to invite the West German Government to contribute armed forces for the common defense of Europe. Everyone was acutely conscious of the resemblance between divided Korea and divided Germany, and of the possibility that an attack might be made on Western Germany. In 1955, Western Germany was made a full member of NATO.

By 1964 the growing military strength of the United States and the West European Powers, together with the relaxation of tension with the Soviet Union following the Test-Ban Treaty, had led to noticeable signs of disintegration in NATO. Its future utility was regarded with growing doubt; but there was no doubt that in its day it had played a great role in saving Europe from communist invasion.

European Union

The dream of a political union of Europe is as old as the Roman Empire. In modern times Hitler tried to unite Europe under his dictatorship. Among the free peoples of Europe the dream takes the form of a United States of Europe, with some kind of federal government. There are, however, many obstacles in the path of European union, ranging from ancestral hatreds to commercial trade barriers that powerful interests demand as protection against competition.

On the other hand, there are forces pushing the Europeans toward political union.

The most conspicuous pressure toward union after World War II was the necessity for common defense. Defense requires more than a unified military force. In the long run defense demands a great increase in the efficiency of European production. And that calls for political union.

In the United States one of the main reasons for high production per man-year is the political union of the states. Under the federal union, the states are forbidden to raise trade barriers against one another's products. Although this prohibition is often evaded, the evasions are of little effect compared with the customs barriers and the change of money between the states of Europe. Another advantage of the political union of the United States is that the Federal Government is strong enough to make and enforce laws against monopoly. These laws too are often evaded, but there has been notably less monopoly in the United States than in Europe. Trade barriers and monopoly long worked together in Europe to waste the energy of the people.

In Europe, it has long been recognized that if the shackles could be loosened, production might be greatly increased. Military costs would be easier to bear. Living conditions would improve. European statesmen were well aware of the strong reasons for trying to build a United States of Europe.

The Coal and Steel Community

A plan for united political control over the steel and coal industries of Europe was proposed by Robert Schuman, the French Foreign Minister, in May, 1950. The treaty establishing the European Community for Coal and Steel was signed April 18, 1951, by France, the Federal Republic of Germany, Italy, Belgium, the Netherlands, and Luxembourg.

The purposes of the Schuman Plan were: first, to improve the efficiency of coal and steel production in Europe; and second, to create a regional program of great economic importance in which France and Germany would work together as partners, and so might learn to forget old hatreds and become friends.

Efficiency was sought by enlarging the market area and by prohibiting monopoly practices. After a period of gradual adjustment, the trade barriers would disappear, and coal and steel could be shipped from one place to another inside the Community wherever the cost and price relationships called for them to go. This freedom would kill off the most inefficient producers and enlarge the operations of the more efficient ones. But it would not work if they should arrange a cartel or other monopoly scheme to prevent the free flow of trade.

The Community was authorized to forbid monopoly, and to fine any company that is convicted of practicing it. In order to exercise the power of enforcing an antimonopoly law, the Community was equipped with a real government, consisting of a High Authority of nine members, a Consultative Committee, an Assembly, a Council of Ministers, and a Court. The Court has power to reverse the decisions of other bodies in the Community for exceeding their authority. As a whole the Community became a true federal government, superior to the six member states, within the field of the laws governing coal and steel.

By 1957 the High Authority was able to report that practically all the old trade barriers had been removed. Steel production, which had been lagging before 1952, had increased 36 percent in five years, considerably faster than that of Britain or the United States.

Meanwhile the Community was powerfully reinforced by the addition of two other organizations, the Common Market and Euratom.

The Common Market and Euratom

Three years after the establishment of the European Community for Coal and Steel, Belgium, the Netherlands, and Luxembourg proposed to France, Germany, and Italy the extension of similar agreements to cover trade in general and the development of atomic energy. The foreign ministers of the six countries met in June, 1955, and began discussions that led to the signing of two new treaties on March 25, 1957. One of these established the European Economic Community, known as the Common Market; and the other the Atomic Energy Community, or Euratom.

Each of these organizations was given a form similar to that of the Community for Coal and Steel, with separate executive commissions but with the same Assembly, Council, and Court acting for all three.

Euratom is similar in form but is comparatively simple because there are no great vested interests in atomic energy to be disturbed by the abolition of trade barriers. Euratom handles importation of atomic fuels, promotes research and training, helps private companies plan for building atomic power plants, sets standards for health and safety, and guards against use of atomic fuels for military or criminal purposes.

Euratom keeps in close touch with the United Nations International Atomic Energy Agency, especially on such problems as international control of dangerous nuclear materials.

The prosperity of the six members of the Common Market was soon growing notably faster than that of other Western nations, including Great Britain and the United States. In 1961 Great Britain, Denmark, Norway, and Ireland applied for full membership in the Common Market. Shortly afterward Switzerland, Sweden, and Austria applied for associate membership. These proposals, however fell to the ground in January, 1963, when President Charles de Gaulle of France vetoed the admission of Great Britain.

Meanwhile, an agreement was negotiated between the Common Market and eighteen African countries for economic cooperation and trade. A remarkable feature of this agreement was a provision allowing the underdeveloped states to maintain tariffs against the European members so that the former's infant industries and balance of payments might be protected.

European Convention for the Protection of Human Rights

This convention was signed by fifteen European states in 1950. It provides for the rights most clearly needed in modern Europe, such as free elections not too long delayed; protection of life, liberty, due process of law; religious freedom; freedom of assembly and expression; and fair treatment of aliens.

A commission that hears and judges complaints has been established in Strasbourg, and there is also a special court to handle difficult cases. Any citizen of a member state can complain of a violation of his rights under the Convention. The commission has only moral powers to enforce its decisions. Its effectiveness lies in preventing unfair treatment rather than in correcting it. In some cases member governments have changed their laws to conform to the

Convention; Norway changed that part of its constitution which interfered with religious freedom. A regional convention of this kind can be highly effective because of the wide agreement on principles existing among the free nations of a region such as Europe.

The Western Pacific

The settlement of the war with Japan was not a responsibility of the UN, but of the fifty-four nations that had been on the winning side. In 1947 the United States proposed a peace conference, but the plan fell through because the Soviet Union refused to cooperate. Finally, in 1950, President Truman decided to go ahead and make peace if possible, even without the Soviets. He appointed John Foster Dulles to negotiate with Japan and with the Allies. The result was the Peace Conference at San Francisco in 1951, where the Soviet efforts to prevent the signing of the peace were unsuccessful. Japan signed the treaty with forty-eight other nations.

The attack in Korea and Chinese aid to the communists in Indochina roused fears of a massive communist drive against Southeast Asia and the islands of the Western Pacific. As a result of these danger signs, in 1954 Mr. Dulles, by then the United States Secretary of State, proposed a Pacific regional defense treaty somewhat like NATO. A conference was held in Manila in September.

The only Asian countries to take part were the Philippines, Thailand, and Pakistan. The other members of the Conference were Australia, France, New Zealand, the United Kingdom, and the United States. Many Asians were suspicious of these other partners in Asian defense, wondering if they might have imperialistic designs of their own. In order to meet these suspicions the Pacific Charter, adopted at the Conference, pledges all the members to promote the independence "of all countries whose people desire it and are able to undertake its responsibilities."

The Conference also adopted a Southeast Asia Collective Defense Treaty in which the parties agreed to unite in defense of any member subjected to attack, or of any other area that the members should unanimously agree to include in their common defense line. A protocol to this treaty specially mentioned Laos, Cambodia, and the non-communist part of Vietnam, the three states of Indochina, as coming under the protection of the agreement, but stressing that the members would take action on the territory of these states only with their consent.

The treaty emphasized the duty of the members to co-operate not only in defense but in economic development, and there has been some modest but effective SEATO activity in this latter field. The bulk of the economic growth in the treaty area, however, has been based on aid from the United States; important help has also come from the United Nations and from the Colombo Plan.

The Colombo Plan is a regional agreement for technical assistance that was started by members of the British Commonwealth, but from the first it has welcomed other free Asian countries. It works in cooperation with the United States aid program and the technical assistance program of the UN. In economic problems as well as in those of collective security many Asian countries are struggling with conditions that invite aggression and that can be corrected only by a long process of upbuilding.

The Middle East

In order to guard the peace in the Middle East, several of the countries along the northern border decided to form a regional organization, and an agreement was signed on February 24, 1955, at Baghdad, Iraq, by Turkey, Iraq, Iran, Pakistan, and the United Kingdom. This agreement was known as the Baghdad Pact, but in 1958 Iraq, after a sudden revolution, ceased to take part in the organization. In 1959 the name was changed to Central Treaty Organization, or CENTO. The United States has from the first taken a keen interest in this organization, and is a member of several of its working committees.

Aside from the coordination of defense measures, CENTO has also begun to work toward more rapid development of the resources of the region. Mutual technical assistance is organized in agriculture, public health, and scientific research; and special emphasis is laid on transport and communications between the member states, which are separated by much mountainous and desert country. One of the first projects was a railway link between Turkey and Iran, avoiding the roundabout route through Soviet territory. Another was a microwave radio transmission system three thousand miles long—the longest in the world—from Ankara in Turkey to Karachi in Pakistan. CENTO is also cooperating with ICAO in supplying modern aids to air navigation through this difficult stretch of territory.

The Organization of American States

The regional organization of the Western Hemisphere has been a natural result of the liberation, more than a century ago, of groups of European colonies, born in weakness and needing the strength of union. First the English colonies after gaining their independence joined to form the United States. Then, in 1826, Simón Bolívar, the great Liberator of the Spanish colonies, called the First Congress of American States at Panama City. Delegates came from Colombia, Central America, Peru, and Mexico, and signed a "Treaty of Perpetual Union."

In the Monroe Doctrine (1823) the United States with the informal backing of British sea power warned the European Holy Alliance, led by Russia, not to try any new colonization in the Americas. For more than a century the Monroe Doctrine was a one-sided defense of the continent. The Latin-American countries regarded the United States with suspicion, fearing that in warning the Europeans to keep out, it was merely reserving the Western Hemisphere for its own imperialistic ambitions.

These suspicions were increased in the early years of the present century, when several Caribbean republics failed to pay their debts and the European creditors threatened to land soldiers to enforce payment. President Theodore Roosevelt feared that the Europeans, once ensconced, might decide to stay. He therefore decided to land United States forces and take over the collection of taxes until the debts were properly covered. The Latin-American nations resented having the United States act as continental policemen.

President Herbert Hoover abandoned the intervention policy, and the feeling of the Latin Americans toward the

United States began to improve. Further improvement of relations during the administrations of President Franklin Roosevelt and President Truman led to the formal establishment of the Organization of American States in 1948.

For many years there had been developing an organization of the American republics, originally designed for the promotion of commerce among the nations of the hemisphere. The first meeting for this purpose was held in Washington in 1889–90, and others were held in later years at which the organization was gradually developed. It was governed by a Governing Board, made up at first of the U. S. Secretary of State and the Washington ambassadors of the other members, and later composed of special delegates chosen by the member countries. Its headquarters staff was called the Pan American Union, and was housed in a monumental building of that name in Washington.

In 1947 at Rio de Janeiro the American states signed the Inter-American Treaty of Reciprocal Assistance, which later served in part as model for the North Atlantic Treaty of 1949. At Bogotá in 1948 they adopted a new Charter establishing their association as the Organization of American States, with the Pan American Union as its secretarial body. The main assembly of the Organization, called the Conference, meets about every five years to settle general policies. A Council, formerly the Governing Board of the Pan American Union, manages the Organization's routine affairs.

Like the UN, the OAS has certain dependent agencies that give technical services to the members in economic, legal, and cultural fields. It also has a number of specialized organizations affiliated with it, such as the Pan American Institute of Geography and History, and institutions for the protection of women and children, and for the development of agriculture. These agencies are coordinated by the Pan American Union, and also cooperate with the corresponding agencies of the UN.

One of the OAS affiliates is the Inter-American Development Bank, founded in April, 1959, to provide capital for private and public projects in the American republics.

The Pan American Sanitary Bureau, established in 1902, is the oldest international public health agency in the world. It now acts as secretariat of the Pan American Health

Organization, which on one hand is a specialized agency of OAS and on the other acts as regional organization of WHO. The work of PAHO has been rapidly expanding until its budget has become larger than that of OAS. It works in three main fields: the fight against infectious diseases; general public health; and the education of health workers.

PAHO is promoting campaigns against malaria, smallpox, yellow fever, yaws, syphilis, polio, rabies, leprosy, and bubonic plague. In these campaigns it works closely with UNICEF and the UN Technical Assistance program, as well as with United States agencies.

The mosquito called Aëdes Aegypti, which is the usual carrier of yellow fever, has been the subject of a war of extermination since 1915, when the Rockefeller Foundation launched a campaign to eliminate yellow fever from the world. Good progress was made in Brazil and some other countries. Bolivia in 1941 announced that it was entirely free of the Aegypti mosquito. But it was evident that no lasting victory could be won unless this mosquito could be totally exterminated in the Americas all the way from the southern United States to Buenos Aires. Accordingly, the Pan American Sanitary Board undertook to coordinate the campaign, with the goal of the extermination of all Aëdes Aegypti mosquitoes from the Western Hemisphere by 1966.

Immediately after the great earthquake in Chile in May, 1960, the Pan American Sanitary Bureau reported airlifting to the stricken country half a million doses of smallpox vaccine and other donated medicines, including gangrene antitoxin and various antibiotics.

The plague is carried by ground squirrels and other small wild animals in many American countries, including the United States. PAHO provides consulting experts to advise on control of these plague-carrying animals.

Another important health program has been the development of a special low-cost food for children in Central America, where undernourishment is widespread. The new food, called Incaparina, is a high-protein mixture of cottonseed meal, corn or rice, sorghum, calcium carbonate, yeast, and vitamin A. It is readily accepted by the children as well as the adults and produces extraordinary improvement in their health.

The Inter-American Institute of Agricultural Sciences is carrying on a series of experiments in the use of radioactive materials in agriculture. A field near Turrialba, Costa Rica, with banks of earth around it to control the radiation, is planted with coffee, bananas, cacao, and other crops to be bombarded with gamma rays, to stimulate the development of new varieties, some of which might be of great value.

In 1960 the United States Congress authorized a special contribution in aid of an expanded program of development in Latin America. In 1961 President Kennedy, with the heads of the other American States, proclaimed an Alliance for Progress, to accelerate economic and social development. The member states laid special emphasis on social reform, chiefly in the channeling of the larger incomes into productive investment instead of wasteful luxuries, and in raising the incomes of the masses of the people, especially on the farms.

The United Nations Economic Commission for Latin America is also pressing for the social reforms necessary for development. It is in a position, through the United Nations, to urge reforms in the trade policies of the richer countries, reforms such as a reduction of trade barriers that hamper the export of manufactured or semi-processed commodities from the developing nations.

Bypassing the UN

With new regional agreements being built up, a great amount of negotiation goes on outside the UN. Friends of the UN often criticize the Powers for "bypassing" the UN, and express the fear that the UN may wither away. The smaller nations in the Assembly are naturally concerned when the Great Powers discuss matters in special conferences where the rest of the nations have no chance to give their opinions or cast their votes.

On the other hand, Article 33 of the Charter directs the members to try to settle their disputes first of all by "negotiation, enquiry, mediation, conciliation, arbitration, judicial settlement, resort to regional agencies or arrangements, or other peaceful means of their own choice." In other words, you must try to avoid appealing to the UN Security Council or the Assembly, but if all other attempts at peaceful settlement fail, then come in and let the world organization judge.

The question about bypassing is a common feature of any system of organizations on more than one level. In human affairs generally, some matters are settled by the family, some by the village or town, some by a country or province, others by a nation or by a regional group of nations or by the human race organized in the United Nations. The exact level where a problem is best handled is often not clear. Continual disputes about "states' rights" are a characteristic of federal governments; continual disputes about "domestic jurisdiction," nationalism, and regionalism may be expected in the UN.

The main principles for understanding such disputes seem fairly clear.

Nationalism, for instance, is the feeling of a people that they are by rights a nation and ought to have their own "sovereignty." They feel oppressed if some other nation rules them. The revolt against colonialism excites the feeling of nationalism, now especially strong in Asia and Africa.

Nationalism is not a form of madness. If people have language, customs, and traditions in common they can settle many questions among themselves better than any other people can do it for them. They should be encouraged to do so, provided they do not disturb their neighbors too much.

Regionalism, in the same way, is the feeling of the nations in one part of the world that they have certain regional problems in common, and that they have some principles and standards in common that may outweigh their differences. Such feelings lead the nations to make regional agreements. This way of solving problems also makes sense, provided the region does not form an alliance to conquer the rest of the world.

The United Nations is based on the feeling that all human beings are the same in some ways and therefore need an organization in which they can act as one on matters in which they agree as members of the human race.

Such matters may include at least the desire to avoid total atomic desolation, and a general desire to promote some kinds of human rights and to raise the level of living. These are the general purposes of the vast majority of sane people. But whether some particular action is best planned on a worldwide scale or in some smaller unit depends on its special character.

The natural principles of human action in large or small groups are fairly plain. But the boundaries between one level of action and the next are apt to be hazy and clouded by the selfish interests of one nation or another. It is only to be expected that people will always argue about where the nation or the region leaves off and the proper field of the United Nations begins.

— 9 —

DISARMAMENT

The idea of an international agreement to reduce military forces was first proposed at a peace conference called by the Czar of Russia in 1899. Modern science was developing big guns and steel-clad warships, and these seemed so costly and dangerous that something would have to be done to put a limit on them. From then on the cost and danger have grown until the most advanced hydrogen and cobalt bomb offers the human race the possibility of killing all or nearly all the living things in the world by the poisoned earth and air left over from a short atomic war. The necessity of avoiding suicide is known to all the world, but how to do it is not so simple.

Meanwhile the world is spending about 120,000 million dollars per year for military activities which is 8 or 9 percent of the world's total production of goods and services.

The Peace Conference of 1899 appointed a committee of experts to study the reduction of armies and navies. The committee reported that no agreement was possible at that time.

Another peace conference in 1907 agreed to prohibit the use of poison in war but did not try to agree on arms reduction.

After World War I the question was more urgent. The victorious Allies disarmed Germany, and decided to put a disarmament clause in the Covenant of the League of Nations, which they were writing along with the peace

154

treaty. Accordingly, Article 8 of the League Covenant provided that the League Council should make plans for arms reduction and offer them to the members for their signature. When these plans were adopted the members would promise to exchange "full and frank information on the scale of their armaments, their naval and air programmes and the condition of such of their industries as are adaptable to warlike purposes." A commission was appointed to advise the League on how to bring about the desired agreements.

In December, 1920, the commission advised that arms reduction at that time would be premature. A new commission was appointed in 1921, which came up with some further steps in the attempt to think out the disarmament problem.

By 1923, then, the main elements of a workable disarmament plan had been named, although naming them was far from being the same as getting the nations to agree to them. These are the main essentials:

1. Full disclosure. No country can have military secrets, or the other countries will be afraid to disarm.

2. Full membership. Every country big enough to be dangerous must be a member of the agreement.

3. Collective security, as it is now called. If any country is attacked the others must be bound by a promise to give immediate help without further argument.

4. Judgment. Some recognized authority must have the information and the means to give an immediate judgment saying which nation is the attacker and which is the victim.

All the arguments since 1923 have consisted of repeating the demand for these essentials in one form of words or another, and finding that some country was determined to leave out some necessary feature. Since that would open a loophole through which an aggressor might draw a sudden bead on his innocent victim, the insistence on the loophole has naturally led to disagreement.

After 1923 the nations of Europe saw little hope that the world could soon agree on a disarmament treaty. As a stopgap they tried regional peace agreements, such as, for instance, the Locarno Pacts. But in 1932 a great conference of sixty-one nations met at Geneva. In addition to fifty-six League members, the United States and four other nonmembers were there.

The Geneva Conference agreed on prohibiting certain weapons such as bombs dropped from airplanes or balloons. It agreed on the principles of arms limitation, on international supervision of the arms business, and on publicity of arms budgets. But it did not find a practical way to get the nations to act on these principles.

Soon afterward, Japan and Germany resigned from the League of Nations. Then in 1935, when Germany started drafting men for its new army, the League gave up trying to promote disarmament. Hitler was planning conquest. For the time being it was too dangerous for anyone to disarm.

It is sometimes said that it takes two to make a quarrel. This saying is true of nations only provided there are no aggressors. It takes only one nation to march over the border for the purpose of conquering its neighbor. So long as anyone who loves freedom has the means of resistance, there will be war if any one nation starts a military aggression.

On the other hand, if all the freedom-loving nations of the world were so completely disarmed that they could offer no resistance, an aggressor could take them over without a war. This is what the aggressor nations mean by their love of peace. Hitler, for instance, spoke often of his deep desire for peace, meaning that when he decided to march he hoped there would be no resistance. Aggressors are strongly convinced that it takes two to make a quarrel, and that if any nation resists their aggression that nation is a warmonger and is guilty of all the blood of those who suffer.

In 1935, when Hitler was building up his armies and talking of his love for peace, the other nations were afraid of what he might be planning to do. They were too much disturbed to disarm, though at the time not enough disturbed to start a heavy rearmament program. It will always happen that if the peace-loving Powers believe that any strong Power is dreaming of military conquests, they will be afraid to disarm and may on the contrary build up their armaments.

What use, then, is there in talking about disarmament year after year, and conference after conference, when everyone knows there are unspoken conditions in the argument that make it hopeless? The use is in the fact that conditions change, and the long years of discussion will help to bring on the needed change, if war should be postponed long enough.

By talking, the nations make clear to themselves and to any possible aggressor the necessary terms of peace and of disarmament as they are now understood. Much of the work of describing these necessary terms was done before 1923, but many details are still not clear. Some details may be less necessary than others. They might be sacrificed in bargaining, to gain agreement on more essential points. No free nation wants to demand or to endure any more international control than is really necessary to get the result. Long and seemingly hopeless argument is hammering out the terms that some day may be accepted.

What would make any aggressor willing to accept conditions that would forever disarm his power to conquer his neighbor? This is the key question of the mid-twentieth century. It has several answers.

If any leaders who want to conquer the world should be convinced that the devastation of a war would leave them fatally shattered, a pressure will be set up in their minds toward giving up the dream of a short, easy, victorious war.

When the leaders who dream of conquest try to lull their victims by talk of peace and fail to get the victims to disarm, their confidence is temporarily shaken, and they show it by being unusually polite. If this condition continues for a long time, if the free nations continue powerfully armed, the dream of conquest may gradually fade. Then the practical advantages in agreeing to a real disarmament may begin to appeal to men who had previously neglected them.

There is evidence that the most influential leaders of the Great Powers in the United Nations are well aware that a nuclear war would be suicidal.

The principle of practical restraint can be easily illustrated by a bit of history that is now too old to carry any hard feeling. About a thousand years ago the Norsemen found profit in raiding the coasts of Britain. Sometimes they were successful, and sometimes the inhabitants killed them and nailed their hides to the church doors. In those days any agreement for a lasting peace would have seemed impossible. But as time went on, military raids on the British coasts ceased to be profitable adventures, and the Scandinavians forgot the whole idea. There is no raider so fierce that he may not quiet down if he finds there is no profit in the business.

Another reason for hope is the well-known fact that subversion in our time is a powerful technique of conquest. All modern aggressors count more or less on persuasion, the technique of the big lie, and the use of dupes for infiltration of the victim's institutions. The peace-loving nations that hope to resist aggression also count heavily on subverting the power of aggression by campaigns of truth. One of the best hopes of military peace is the belief on each side that it has a chance to win by propaganda, undermining the other side's will to resist.

Propaganda, for a Big Power, is cheaper and safer than shooting. Any aggressor who has a deep faith that he can win the world by propaganda and subversion would be glad to do it in that inexpensive way instead of by the simpler but more risky use of armed force against well-armed opponents.

If that be true, the hope of forever postponing a new world war and of ultimately abolishing aggressive weapons is not entirely an insane hope.

The UN and the Atom Bomb

The UN Charter authorized the Security Council to make plans for the regulation of armaments and to submit them to the members. The Assembly was also authorized to "consider the principles governing disarmament," and to make recommendations about them.

Then a few weeks after the signing of the Charter the atomic bomb came into action, and the disarmament question was stepped up to a consideration of the life or death of the human race.

On November 15, 1945, Canada, the United Kingdom, and the United States proposed a UN commission to study the control of the atom. In December the Soviet Union joined in sponsoring the proposal. It was adopted unanimously at the first session of the General Assembly in January, 1946, and the Atomic Energy Commission was established, consisting of all members of the Security Council together with Canada when not a member of the Council.

The Atomic Energy Commission soon became deadlocked. The U.S.S.R. would not allow unlimited inspection, saying that it infringed national sovereignty. It also demanded an agreement to abolish atomic weapons as a first step toward the adoption of a control system. The Western Powers insisted that safeguards against cheating were the necessary condition for any disarmament agreement.

In December, 1946, the General Assembly recommended that the Security Council make plans for reducing ordinary armaments. It also recommended an early start toward organizing the UN police force as provided in the Charter. At that time it was commonly believed that collective security, a necessary base for general disarmament, could be had by organizing UN armed forces to overawe any aggressor.

The Commission for Conventional Armaments was established by the Security Council in 1947, but it too bogged down. The Assembly abolished both commissions and in January, 1952, created a new Disarmament Commission, with the same membership as the Atomic Energy Commission, to consider both atomic and ordinary arms restriction together. A subcommittee of five Powers—Canada, France, the U.S.S.R., the United Kingdom, and the United States—was later established to carry on talks in private.

In July, 1955, President Eisenhower and the heads of the British, French, and Soviet governments held a "summit meeting" in Geneva, and arranged for a conference of their foreign ministers to take place in October. No final agreement resulted from either of these meetings.

The Disarmament Commission reported to the Assembly in November, 1955. A serious stumbling block had arisen:

the disclosure—agreed by all parties—that there was no known way of detecting hidden stores of atomic weapon materials, such as plutonium.

The subcommittee made little progress during the next year, for the Western Powers could not agree to the Soviet demands for immediate prohibition of nuclear weapons and the liquidation of all military bases in foreign states.

Beginning in 1955 there was some discussion of the possibility of partial disarmament as a first step, but no agreement was reached. In 1957 the General Assembly urged the Powers to reach an early agreement to stop nuclear arms testing. It also urged them to halt the production of fissionable material for weapons, to cut down their stocks of such weapons, to proceed with general disarmament under proper safeguards, and to study how the use of outer space might be limited to peaceful purposes.

The United States, Britain, and the Soviet Union all voluntarily stopped the testing of atomic and hydrogen bombs, which had begun to spread measurable quantities of radioactive fallout. Meanwhile long and patient discussions were going on at Geneva on many technical problems that would have to be handled in any successful disarmament plan. There was, for instance, an attempt to agree on how to prevent surprise attack. There were long and encouraging talks on the cessation of nuclear tests, leading to an agreement that the obligation to stop the tests and the establishment of the control systems must go hand in hand. There was a broad coming together on the general shape of a control organization, to be headed by a seven-nation commission. The negotiators agreed on the principle that nuclear explosions for peaceful purposes could be allowed under carefully prescribed conditions and under international observation. Many noncontroversial clauses for a proposed treaty were drafted; it was agreed that the treaty would come into force when ratified by the United Kingdom, the United States, and the U.S.S.R., but would be open to all nations with the hope of making it worldwide.

During 1958 and early 1959 evidence gradually piled up that the Atomic Powers were becoming more and more anxious about the growing danger of world suicide, and more serious in wanting to stop the arms race.

Finally on September 7, 1959, the UN representatives of Britain, France, the Soviet Union, and the United States sent a joint letter to the Secretary-General, notifying him that the four Powers had organized a new ten-member disarmament committee, consisting of equal numbers of socialist and nonsocialist states. The other six members were: Bulgaria, Canada, Czechoslovakia, Italy, Poland, and Romania.

The four Powers acknowledged that according to the Charter, "disarmament matters are of world-wide interest and concern. Accordingly, ultimate responsibility . . . rests with the United Nations. The setting up of the disarmament committee in no way diminishes or encroaches upon the United Nations responsibilities in this field. In setting up this committee, the special responsibility resting on the great powers to find a basis for agreement is taken into account."

The four Powers promised that the new committee would report its discussions to the UN Disarmament Commission, and arrangements were made to use the UN services and facilities in Geneva.

On September 10 the Secretary-General called a meeting of the Disarmament Commission, which had meanwhile been enlarged to include all the UN members, under a resolution passed in 1958. The Commission unanimously voted to welcome the resumption of negotiations, and expressed the hope that the ten-nation committee would find a useful basis for United Nations action.

On September 18, 1959, Mr. Nikita Khrushchev, who was visiting the United States, addressed the General Assembly of the United Nations.

The Soviet leader proposed a four-year program of complete and general disarmament. He called for the total abolition of all armies, navies, and air forces, of general staffs and war ministries, and the closing of all military establishments, the destruction of all nuclear weapons, and the use of rockets only for peaceful exploration of outer space. He said the Soviet Union would be prepared to join with other nations in economic aid to the underdeveloped countries.

The General Assembly's Political and Security Committee began a full-scale discussion of disarmament on October 9, 1959, and two formal declarations were considered, one from the United Kingdom and the other from the Soviet Union.

A point often made in the debate, especially by the smaller nations, was their pleasure at the thought of economic development taking the place of the arms race, as well as their insistence that the Big Powers were responsible for finding a way to avoid universal destruction.

As the 1959 session of the Assembly ended, there was a general feeling that disarmament was not as hopeless as it had appeared during the first twelve years after World War II.

The Eighteen-Nation Committee

On the 20th of December, 1961, the Assembly established a new eighteen-nation committee to sit at Geneva and negotiate on disarmament on the basis of certain agreed principles proposed jointly by the Soviet Union and the United States. The members were: the Soviet Union, Bulgaria, Czechoslovakia, Poland, Romania; the United States, the United Kingdom, France, Italy, Canada; Brazil, Burma, Ethiopia, India, Mexico, Nigeria, Sweden, and the United Arab Republic.

France has refused to attend meetings of the Committee, and it is sometimes called the Seventeen-Nation Committee.

The Committee met in March, 1962, and took up the question of general and complete disarmament, which had been proposed by Mr. Khrushchev. The Soviet delegate presented a proposed draft of a treaty, and in April the United States also presented an outline of a possible treaty.

Both drafts provided for disarmament by stages. The details were carefully drafted by each side to make sure that in the scaling down of armaments neither one would be placed at a disadvantage. The proposals included provisions for verification of each stage before starting the next. Discussion brought out the fact that "complete" disarmament did not mean the abolition of armed forces necessary for internal security. Such forces of course would not involve nuclear weapons.

The Khrushchev proposal of complete disarmament within four years was an appealing one to many of the new UN members who had a well-justified horror of a possible nuclear holocaust, but who had no technical knowledge of the extreme difficulty of "cramming the atom back into the bottle."

For example, there is so far no acceptable way of making sure that a reserve stock of atom bombs is not hidden in an abandoned mine in some remote territory.

Accordingly, while it is politically necessary to devote much time and technical work at Geneva to a solemn discussion of a treaty of total disarmament, the fact is that no such overall treaty can be agreed upon in the immediate future. Progress can be made toward reducing the danger of nuclear war, and it is being made, but not along that road.

Fortunately, after the unsuccessful attempt by the Soviet Union to place a decisive installation of nuclear missiles in Cuba in the summer of 1962 without being prematurely discovered, the cold war began to thaw. Under the new conditions the disarmament problem took on a new form. The worldwide moral pressure on the nuclear Powers to stop polluting air and sea with test bombs began to show practical effects.

The Test-Ban Treaty

One of the first actions of the Eighteen-Nation Committee had been to appoint the United States, the Soviet Union, and the United Kingdom as a subcommittee to negotiate a test-ban treaty.

Much time was spent in arguing about how to check on underground shocks recorded by earthquake stations as having occurred in the Soviet Union. Were they underground nuclear tests or only earthquakes? The United States wanted a system of recording stations located in the Soviet territory, manned by scientists who would have the right to inspect any point where a shock occurred.

The communists wanted only a limited number of such inspections, if any. As always, the roadblock was the strong communist objection to outside observation.

Finally in August, 1962, the United States proposed an alternate treaty, to cover tests in the air, under water, or in outer space. These can all be observed without sending anyone to inspect on the spot. Underground tests, in any case, do not pollute air, sea, or space with radioactive fallout, and there is not so much point in trying to abolish them. The Soviet Union at first rejected the partial test ban, and discussions continued on possible inspection arrangements.

The General Assembly passed resolutions late in 1962 urging that the nuclear Powers agree on a treaty permanently stopping all kinds of nuclear tests on the 1st of January, 1963, but the Assembly provided no realistic answer to the problem raised by the communist refusal of any practical inspection system.

Meanwhile in the United States the Arms Control and Disarmament Agency was studying the many complex problems involved in United States commitment to a test ban. The Agency's experts studied the probable effects of a partial test ban on the balance of military power, the problem of how to maintain a readiness to test in case the Soviets should breach the treaty, and the question of what harm could be done by continuance of underground testing. Probably no treaty ever signed by the United States represented so much careful scientific investigation as the 1963 test-ban treaty.

Finally, in July, 1963, the treaty was agreed upon by the Soviet Union, the United States, and the United Kingdom. Nearly all the nations of the world expressed their enthusiastic relief by adding their signatures to the treaty, with the notable exceptions of France and Communist China. Underground tests are not covered by the treaty, but the pollution of the atmosphere by bomb explosions was stopped.

The Hot Line

After the Cuban crisis, which was settled after several days of dangerous delay, President Kennedy and Chair-

man Khrushchev agreed that they needed a direct telephone line to reduce the danger of war by misunder-
standing. As a result a teletype line, which is always
manned at both ends so that the two heads of state can
get in touch with each other on short notice by day or
night, was established. This is not a voice telephone, since
talking through interpreters could lead to misunderstand-
ing and too-sudden reactions. Each sentence can be examined by interpreters, and questions can be clarified before
a reply is drafted; but the time is reduced to minutes
instead of hours or days. This is a long way from the
situation during the War of 1812 between England and
the United States, in which the battle of New Orleans was
fought after the peace treaty had been signed and was on
its way across the sea by sailing vessel.

Another important agreement, more fully described in
Chapter 10, was the resolution prohibiting the placing of
weapons of mass destruction into orbit, which was offered
to the General Assembly by the United States and the
Soviet Union during the 1963 session. On the other hand,
the communist objections to the orbiting of observation
capsules with high-powered cameras, voiced early in 1963,
met with so little support that they were dropped in the
space-law resolutions later that year. So far as disarmament is concerned it is clear that the development of better
inspection techniques will reduce the chief obstacle to the
cutting down of armed forces.

Other Disarmament Proposals

On January 21, 1964, President Johnson sent a mes-
sage to the Geneva Disarmament Conference suggesting
five points on which the United States would like to negotiate.

First he proposed an overall end to the cold war by an
agreement not to use force or the threat of force, or by
aggression, subversion, or the supply of arms to change
national boundaries, to interfere with access to territory,
or to overthrow governments.

Second, he proposed an agreement to build no more
missiles, rockets, or other means of delivering nuclear
bombs.

Third, he proposed a halt in the production of nuclear materials that could be used for war.

Fourth, he proposed a system of observation posts on both sides of the iron curtain to guard against surprise attack or war by miscalculation.

Fifth and finally, the President proposed an agreement to prevent the spread of nuclear weapons to any nations that do not now have them.

Another current topic of discussion is the United States proposal for a "bonfire" of obsolete bombers no longer useful to the Great Powers, but dangerous to peace if sold to smaller countries that have designs on their neighbors.

Some of these proposals have also been put forward by the Soviet Union in one form or another, and in course of time, if the tension continues to ease, some agreements will probably be worked out.

The United States disarmament agency is constantly studying techniques for reducing Soviet objections to specific agreements. Less offensive methods of inspection, through the use of more advanced instruments, are constantly under study. An important topic is the analysis of Soviet budget reporting, in an effort to understand exactly what expenditures are really military. Another topic of vast interest is the discovery of possible actions that would be so beneficial to both sides that great confidence can be placed in an agreement even without inspection. A striking illustration is the gradual stepping down of military expenditures, agreed upon by President Johnson and Chairman Khrushchev during 1963–64. Both sides have plenty of nuclear weapons with which to destroy each other—and most of the world besides—and both can profitably cut down on further stockpiling and use the money for other purposes.

We now have, at last, a practical approach to disarmament. The fact that war between the Great Powers would be suicide is known to all except the Chinese Communist leaders, and they will have time to learn this before they can become a dangerous nuclear Power. The moral pressure of the UN, though it is sometimes ill-informed about practical details, is constantly and usefully applied by the General Assembly through the Eighteen-Nation Committee. So long as the leadership of the nuclear Power is in the hands of men who want to avoid World War III, progress can be expected with some confidence.

As President Kennedy said in an address to the General Assembly in September, 1963: "A test-ban treaty is a milestone, but that is not the millennium. We have not been released from our obligations; we have been given an opportunity. . . . In these and other ways let us move up the steep and difficult path toward comprehensive disarmament, securing mutual confidence through mutual verification, and building the institutions of peace as we dismantle the engines of war."

OUTER SPACE AND THE ATOM

The principle that friendship among people of alien cultures is most readily built by working in cooperation for some valuable material achievement may well find an important application in the exploration of space. Here the human race can look out upon something vast, cold, and unapproachable except through the gates of abstract science. If we can begin here with reverential awe, we can hope to continue with a growing sense that in the face of this majesty all human disputes are insignificant.

The danger that space exploration would focus on a contest between the Soviet Union and the United States for military advantage could be avoided only if the two antagonists could agree at an early stage that cooperation was the better way. The United Nations provides the meeting ground for the first stages of such an agreement, which if achieved could be one of the greatest successes of its first twenty years.

In December, 1959, the General Assembly debated the subject of outer space for the first time, and adopted without a dissenting voice a resolution creating the United Nations Committee on the Peaceful Uses of Outer Space, made up of twenty-four nations, conspicuously including the Soviet Union and the United States.

The main purposes of this Space Committee, as set forth in the resolution, are to promote international co-operation, and in particular to encourage the nations to carry forward on a permanent basis the space research

168

begun with such cordial worldwide cooperation in the International Geophysical Year. The Committee was directed to encourage the nations to study space problems and exchange scientific information.

In addition, the Space Committee was directed to "study the nature of the legal problems which may arise from exploration of outer space." No one knew much about what these problems would be, but anyone could see that near the earth, traffic control and allocation of radio bands would soon need to be considered by some international agency. In fact, the International Telecommunication Union announced in 1959 the formation of a committee to study the allocation of radio bands for space research. The committee was made up of representatives of Czechoslovakia, France, the U.S.S.R., the United Kingdom, and the United States.

With the founding of the UN Space Committee and the discussion indicating its cordial acceptance by the Soviet Union and the United States, all the delegations seemed to feel a cool breath of fresh air and the possible dawn of peace. All the nations, great and small, gave a sigh of relief, for though the danger of universal madness and suicide had not been abolished, human sanity had broken through in a new direction that could be a path to peace.

With this breakthrough the importance of the United Nations itself rose to a new level. In particular, the feeling long held by many friends of the UN, that in the end that body must be sovereign of the open spaces of the world, broke through into the sky with the hint of UN sovereignty in outer space.

In September, 1961, President Kennedy offered the United Nations a program for space cooperation. He called for the establishment of law and order among all nations venturing into space; for scientific cooperation in the exchange of information; for worldwide weather reporting and study; and for a global system of communication satellites. This program was unanimously approved by the General Assembly on December 4, 1961.

Space Law

The first principles of space law to be agreed upon were that international law, including the UN Charter, must apply to outer space and to celestial bodies, and that no nation could claim any sovereign rights in space or on any celestial body.

In the debate on space law several communist states voiced the Soviet objections to the American observation satellites, saying that they were a form of military aggression in the same class with the flight of high U-2 planes over Soviet territory, which the United States had discontinued after Soviet protests.

In effect, the already recognized rule that no country can own any part of outer space necessarily applies to the space around the Earth where the satellites have their orbits. National sovereignty, therefore, can extend upward only to the top of the atmosphere in which airplanes can fly. Above that, anything flying is in outer space and is not trespassing on the sovereignty of the nation down below. Since these relationships are imposed by the laws of nature, any attempt to extend national sovereignty to the space beyond the atmosphere will necessarily fail. World opinion is likely to be more in favor of open skies than of a theoretical extension of sovereignty into the near parts of space where the satellites play, since the purpose of such an extension could only be to protect aggressive preparations in expansionist countries.

In October, 1963, the Assembly endorsed an agreement announced by the United States and the U.S.S.R. that promised not to station in space any nuclear weapons or other weapons of mass destruction. There was some comment on the fact that this agreement included no provision for inspection to prevent cheating. But in the friendly atmosphere generated by the three-month-old Test-Ban Treaty, the agreement was regarded as hopeful.

There were some practical grounds for hope that the agreement might hold. Both the Soviet Union and the United States are known to have more than enough nuclear missiles to destroy each other. This fact would seem to reduce the value of having still more weapons orbiting in the sky. Moreover, they might be difficult to remove safely at some future time if peace should break out.

Other Laws of Space

The 1963 Assembly readily agreed to several practical principles of space law. No country ought to launch anything into space that would interfere with the peaceful use of space by all countries. This is the beginning of a set of traffic laws for the crowded area near the earth. All objects launched into space from any nation's territory, by public or private enterprise, are under the authority of the nation from which they come, and that nation is responsible for their behavior. Damage done by any manmade object launched into space is the responsibility of the nation from which it was launched.

Spaceships and astronauts making a landing in a foreign country are to be well treated and returned promptly to their own country.

The Space Committee was directed to draft these principles into the form of treaties, which will become international law on being accepted by the nations concerned in space activities.

Technical Cooperation in Space

The UN Space Committee has a Technical Subcommittee that works to promote international cooperation in space science. Scientific reports are exchanged through two independent organizations in the field: the Committee on Space Research of the International Council of Scientific Unions (COSPAR), and the World Data Centers for Rockets and Satellites.

The United States space agency, the National Aeronautics and Space Administration (NASA), was directed by the United States Congress to cooperate in space research, and it has made an agreement for this purpose with the Soviet Union. By 1962 it was engaged in cooperative experiments with over sixty other countries. For example it launched a research satellite produced by the Canadian Telecommunications Research Establishment in September, 1962.

A cooperative program promoted by the UN Space Committee is based on a series of vertical sounding rockets to study conditions in the upper atmosphere and the fringes of outer space, especially along the line of the magnetic equator. India led the way in 1963 with a launching site close to that equator.

Many countries all around the world have provided sites for tracking stations to keep in touch with satellites of various kinds.

The Space Committee helps to impress upon the member countries the importance of planning space experiments with the utmost care to avoid the pollution of space with debris that will interfere with future travel or experiments—as, for instance, cutting off light or radio rays from the stars. It is possible to imagine a distant day when the UN sky-cleaning spaceships will sail about a few hundred miles above the earth sweeping up dead satellites and other trash and dumping it over the Arctic Ocean. By a resolution passed in 1961, the UN set up a comprehensive registry of all objects launched into orbit or beyond, and voluntarily reported.

Weather and Communications

The use of satellites with television cameras put the cap on the World Meteorological Organization's system of weather reporting and analysis. With wide pictures of cloud formations from above and reports of conditions on the ground and at various levels in the air, the weather scientist can have a clear understanding of what the atmosphere is doing. With computers to do the mathematics at the speed of lightning, he can learn to recognize the pattern of events and its resemblance to patterns that have occurred before. With this knowledge he may soon be able to make more accurate and more long-range predictions than are now possible.

Several weather satellites are now in orbit; the system is growing rapidly, with the cordial encouragement and advice of the World Meteorological Organization.

Similarly, the success of Telstar and Relay, the American communications satellites, roused worldwide interest and has set off a program for a worldwide system. These satellites, flying so high as to be visible from stations several thousand miles apart, serve as transmitters for radio signals that cannot follow the curvature of the earth, such as television programs. To maintain continuous service it is necessary to have a series of telstars, so that one will be available at all times. The sky may be expected to be well filled with such relaying satellites as time goes on. The coordination of such a system into a practical communications network will, of course, be mainly a work for the International Telecommunication Union. One of the present problems of this Agency is the allocation of radio frequencies for satellite communications in the world system.

Education and Health

The Outer Space Committee is cooperating with UNESCO to organize a system for the training of young scientists in the skills required for work in the exploration of space. It is particularly interested in promoting travel fellowships for students who cannot find the necessary courses of study in their own countries. A subject of growing future importance will be research into the physical and mental health hazards of space travel, and how they may be kept to a minimum.

Peaceful Uses of the Atom

In December, 1953, President Eisenhower addressed the General Assembly of the United Nations. He called attention to the dangers of total destruction by atomic and hydrogen bombs, and suggested a new "Atoms for Peace" plan for easing the suspicions that were preventing agreement on controls.

The President proposed that the Powers having nuclear materials contribute some of them to a pool to be used for the peaceful development of atomic energy. He suggested that the program should be operated by an International Atomic Energy Agency, to be sponsored by the United Nations.

The Soviet Union agreed to negotiate with the United States on the matter but wanted to combine the President's proposal with a ban on atomic weapons, one of the main points of dispute in the disarmament negotiations. It also wanted the new agency to be controlled by the Security Council, where it would be subject to the veto. The United States insisted on keeping it free of such entanglements.

On December 4, 1954, the Assembly unanimously adopted a resolution endorsing the proposed International Atomic Energy Agency and calling for an international conference to study how the peaceful uses of atomic energy might be developed by cooperation among the nations. In 1956 representatives of the twelve nations that already had some atomic resources met from February to April in Washington. The founding statute of the Agency, which includes a provision for inspection to make sure that stocks of nuclear fuel provided by the Agency would not be used for making weapons, was signed by eighty nations in October, 1956. Sterling Cole, of the United States, was appointed Director-General of the Agency. The IAEA opened for business on October 1, 1957, at its headquarters in Vienna. To set it on its way the United States pledged 5,000 kilograms (about 11,000 lbs.) of uranium 235, the Soviet Union pledged 50 kilograms, and other members smaller amounts. Much larger quantities would of course be used every year after the program got fully under way.

Meanwhile, in response to widespread alarm over the dangers of atomic fallout, the Scientific Committee on the Effects of Atomic Radiation was set up to coordinate information obtainable from member countries and from FAO, WHO, UNESCO, and other organizations. Even if a nuclear war can be avoided there will still be a serious question about the disposal of radioactive wastes from atomic power plants. There is some hope of developing new forms of atomic power that will not produce poisonous ashes, particularly if hydrogen power can be harnessed, but for the time being the dangers are a matter for anxious discussion in the United Nations.

The Committee reported to the General Assembly in 1958, reviewing the existing knowledge of the subject. It concluded that all atomic radiation is a menace to health and to heredity. The less there is of it the fewer people will be struck, but there is no harmless level of pollution with radioactive materials. The Assembly asked the Committee to continue studying the situation and to report every year.

The separation of peaceful atomic developments from the weapons problem is designed to contribute to the pressures for a peaceful solution. That is why the proponents of Atoms for Peace refused to accept the proposal to connect it with the discussion of atomic disarmament. As Henry Cabot Lodge, the United States delegate, said in November, 1954:

> Disarmament is one element in the building of peace. At least one other element is a new world outlook which may get us into the habit of working together and thus, eventually, of trusting each other. We think that this "Atoms for Peace" proposal will lead the world away from war because it is a new prism through which we can look at the problems of the world. It is a new place at which to begin.

Technical Cooperation

When the UN held a conference on the Application of Science and Technology for the Benefit of the Less-Developed Areas, in Geneva in February, 1963, the IAEA sent staff representatives who presented papers on the prospects for nuclear power and the uses of radioactive materials. The Agency has also cooperated with WHO, FAO, UNESCO, and other agencies that have an interest of one kind or another in the uses of atomic energy.

The IAEA is of course particularly concerned with the gradual advance of atomic power technology, on which it publishes reports from time to time. Many of the less-developed countries where conventional sources of power are scarce and costly have been disappointed by the high cost of atomic power, especially in small or medium-sized plants, as well as by the necessity of employing highly trained technical experts to run the plants. Experimentation in the advanced countries is, however, reducing the costs, and IAEA is encouraging the training of technicians from many countries.

In 1963 the United States Atomic Energy Commission estimated that ordinary atomic power plants will be able to compete with coal-burning plants in the United States in the 1970's. Breeder plants, which in generating power also transform the inactive form of uranium into usable fuel material, are expected to be competitive in the 1980's. Even in 1964 a study made in the University of California showed that a large atomic plant could be constructed to produce 650 million gallons of fresh water per day from seawater at a practical cost of thirty cents per thousand gallons, together with enough cheap electricity for a modern city of 2,000,000 people. Such an installation, of course, would find a market only in a highly developed or very rich country faced with local water shortage. For smaller plants the costs would be considerably higher, but the prospects for nuclear power in some of the developing countries within the next twenty years are still considered good.

The IAEA has encouraged the formation of study panels of specialists from various member countries to study such matters as the technology of heavy water and the use of nuclear reactors for chemical research. By 1963 about 45 percent of the Agency's member nations had installed research reactors. The Agency offers technical advice on the use of these reactors in training as well as in the development of new knowledge.

At the invitation of the Italian Government, IAEA arranged in 1963 for the establishment of an international center for the study of theoretical physics at Trieste.

Radioactive Materials

When atomic fuel elements are split apart in a reactor, the resulting fragments are not normal elements such as are usually found in nature; in settling down into a final form the fragments give off rays of energy and flying particles. These unstable forms of the various fragment elements are known as radioisotopes. This secondary radiation may continue for a few seconds or for many years. Some of the atoms from a bomb explosion in the atmosphere, such as strontium 90, will last for a long time and settle to the earth, where they are taken up by plants and eaten by people, whose hereditary qualities can be permanently damaged by the ceaseless inner radiation. This is the "fallout" danger. Other radio isotopes can be collected from a reactor or atomic power plant and used, with suitable precautions, in agriculture, medicine, industry, and various kinds of research.

The Atomic Energy Agency is promoting research in the use of radioisotopes. One useful technique is to irradiate male insects; this does not kill them but renders them sterile. Large numbers of sterile males are then released to compete with the normal males and thus deceive the females and reduce the birthrate. Studies of this system of insect control have been sponsored by IAEA in Belgium, El Salvador, Israel, Italy, and Tunisia. By 1962 there were twenty-two contracts for various studies on the use of isotopes in agriculture, of which fourteen were in less-developed member countries.

Radioisotopes are used in industry to provide radiation for hundreds of purposes, such as the sterilization of food products, and the stimulation of chemical reactions that will not otherwise occur. An IAEA survey in 1960 showed that there were already some 900 industrial applications in forty kinds of industry.

The Agency reports that in water engineering, work is being done to trace the movements of underground water in Turkey, and of mud in a lake region in Cambodia. Radioisotopes, if placed into a river or into the bloodstream of an animal, can be traced by detecting their radiations with a Geiger counter.

One of the services offered by IAEA is the distribution of standardized radioisotopes, which can be used in the laboratories of member states to check and calibrate their own radiation-measuring instruments. Accuracy of dosage is important in many uses of radiation, including its medicinal use.

Radiation has long been employed in the treatment of cancer, and rays from radioisotopes are being widely used in medical diagnosis, particularly of tropical diseases. A large part of the Agency's technical assistance work is in the promotion of research on the rapidly developing use of radioisotopes for medical studies, diagnosis, and treatment.

Radiation Poisoning

Radiation comes from the sky in various forms, among which are "cosmic" rays from the sun and from the universe. Many of these can damage living things, especially by changing their genes and thus causing the birth of "sports" or freaks. The invention of X rays and atomic-fission techniques has increased the total radiation, especially in the areas where nuclear work is going on. Severe doses of radiation can cause serious damage to living beings, ranging from bone cancer to death. The IAEA is therefore particularly interested in studying the quantity of man-made radiation that is loose in the world and hunting for ways to reduce and control it. The Agency reports that in 1962 research on radiation poisoning and its treatment was being carried forward under ten contracts with institutions in eight member states. The Agency and WHO held a joint conference on the subject in Vienna in October, 1962.

One of the most important problems in the use of atomic energy is that of the disposal of wastes. The Agency is helping to coordinate the worldwide studies that are being made by many nations to find the least dangerous and harmful ways of disposing of radioactive waste products. Of particular interest is the effect of dumping at sea. It is clear that no nation has a right to pollute the sea with radioactive material without consideration for the general welfare. The United States Atomic Energy Commission Chairman suggested in 1963 that the Agency should maintain a complete record of sea disposals. An IAEA panel has been appointed to draft a code of international law on the dumping of radioactive wastes in the sea. To a lesser degree, it is necessary to take account of the pollution of underground waters if wastes are buried on land.

The Agency is active in the study of safety measures for atomic power plants, and of rules for the safe transport of radioactive materials.

Safeguards Against Military Use

From the first the IAEA was intended to be armed with a strong system of safeguards to guarantee that none of the member states receiving atomic fuels for power plants or research reactors should secretly or openly divert any of these fuels to the production of bombs. Some of the member states have admitted IAEA safe-guard-systems. The United States has opened a few of its reactors to inspection for the purpose of studying how a safeguard-system can best be managed, and in 1963 it announced that where it had direct contracts for atomic plants with other countries it would negotiate with a view to getting them to accept IAEA safeguards. As a whole, while the safeguards against an occasional atomic weapon being manufactured in a small country may not guarantee absolute safety, the possible gains from posses-sion of a small atomic military force would not appear to offer much temptation.

Is the Atom a Blessing or a Curse?

It is, of course, both, like the automobile, the chemical insecticide, and many other products of science and in-vention. If the human race escapes being destroyed in a nuclear war, the United Nations will be entitled to much of the credit. If the sea does not become a dead body of radioactive water, the United Nations will have had much to do with saving it.

If the burgeoning civilizations of the scientific twenty-first century do not run short of power, it may well be because the Atomic Energy Agency of the United Nations has helped to promote a worldwide development of atomic power with safeguards against worldwide spread of atomic weapons. There are also advantages to be found from its use in agriculture, industry, and medicine.

The atom brings both terror and opportunity. Of late years hope has begun to grow in the United Nations that the benefits may prevail over the harmful effects.

— 11 —

THE ORGANIZATION
OF THE UNITED NATIONS

When the League of Nations was founded in 1919, it had an important new feature. The League was designed to be a continuing organization of the nations for peace and progress along every line of action. There had been international organizations for limited purposes, such as the Universal Postal Union. There had been great peace conferences and disarmament conferences, but they met, discussed, passed resolutions, and dissolved. The League was intended to be permanent, carrying on a growing body of tradition that the members would come to treat with respect. The League was destroyed in World War II, but the idea had taken root.

In particular, the people of the United States, more than half of whom had wanted to join the League in 1920, were determined in 1945 to join a new United Nations Organization.

The nations that met at San Francisco early in 1945 came with the purpose of setting up a permanent world organization with a more complete program of work than the League had had. None of them wanted to create a world government, however. For that reason it is not realistic to judge the United Nations by the standards used in classifying governments, such as, for instance, democratic representation, law enforcement, or the taxing power. Instead of hunting for traces of government, it is better to take the organization as it is and see what it is supposed to do, and how it is equipped to do it.

180

The General Assembly

The General Assembly is the central, or principal, organ of the UN and is made up of all the member nations. Each member can send five representatives to the Assembly, but in any case each member has only one vote.

The General Assembly elects its own President and Vice-Presidents for each session. While the Secretary-General is the chief UN official, the President of the Assembly is the most prominent individual in the United Nations while the Assembly is in session. Both these officials have so far been chosen with great care and success and have exerted a powerful influence for the advancement of the UN—an influence based not only on their positions but on their own characters.

The Assembly appoints committees of many kinds to prepare the work for its regular sessions.

The seven main committees discuss items on the agenda and recommend action. Every member nation can have a representative on each of these committees.

There is a General Committee, which recommends what items the Assembly should consider and which organizes its work. This General Committee consists of the President of the Assembly, seventeen Vice-Presidents, and the Chairmen of the seven main committees. There are also special committees to deal with problems such as Korean reunification, the care of refugees, the effects of atomic radiation, or the peaceful uses of outer space.

The General Assembly may consider any question related to peace and security and to the promotion of world prosperity and justice, except matters that are being acted upon by the Security Council, and matters that are strictly the internal affairs of member nations. In practice, if the Security Council votes and action is blocked by a veto, the question is then open for the Assembly to take it up. As for the definition of "internal affairs," there have been many disputes. Powers that hold colonies, for instance, have sometimes taken the position that the affairs of the colonies are internal and not open to UN discussion. The smaller nations, especially those recently freed from colonial status, want to discuss the complaints of dependent territories. The tendency is for the UN to take more and more interest in the dependent areas.

All UN agencies report directly or indirectly to the General Assembly, which may discuss their activities and recommend changes. The Assembly decides important questions—including those on UN organizational matters such as the election of members to the UN or to the Security Council and Trusteeship Council—by a two-thirds vote. All other matters are decided by a simple majority.

The Assembly adopts the general budget of the UN and assesses the members for their shares of the budget according to their ability to pay. Such factors as national income, average income per person, temporary dislocation of national income, and ability to obtain foreign money are taken into consideration. The UN budget for 1964 was about $100,000,000 and the assessments ranged from 33.3 percent of the total for the United States and 13.96 percent for the Soviet Union down to 0.04 percent for several of the small countries such as Haiti and Iceland. The fact that every member has to pay what the Assembly demands or face discipline does not make the Assembly a government. The same power is found in any private club.

The Security Council

The Security Council is made up of eleven members. Five of these are permanent members, being the five Great Powers as of 1945—China, France, the United Kingdom, the United States, and the U.S.S.R. The other six are elected by the General Assembly for two-year terms, three each year.

The original intention was that the Security Council should have a military force at its command, which it could use to keep order among the nations. In signing the Charter, the members agreed to obey the decisions of the Council, which therefore has in theory certain legislative powers within the field of its job as policeman.

In practice, however, the Council has not been able to agree on how to organize a UN police force. Moreover, except in the case of Korea, it has not been able to agree on the use of force. Its legislative powers therefore have

almost dried up. In their place, the Assembly has enlarged its ability to make recommendations, backed only
by moral force, which appears to be more potent than UN
police power.

The Security Council requires a vote of any seven out
of the eleven members to pass a decision on what is called
a "procedural" matter—any internal question not directly
affecting outside interests. "Substantive" matters require
a vote of seven, including all five permanent members.
This is the so-called "veto" of the five Great Powers. If a
member is a party to a dispute, however, it must abstain
from voting; in practice, an abstention by a permanent
member is not regarded as a veto.

Any nation, whether a member of the UN or not, may
bring to the attention of the General Assembly or the
Security Council any dispute that seems likely to lead to a
breach of the peace. Both bodies have wide powers under
the Charter to attempt peaceful methods of settlement before using force or the recommendation of force.

The Council has a right of veto on the admission of
new members to the UN, which it has often used.

The Economic and Social Council (ECOSOC)

ECOSOC is made up of eighteen member states, elected
by the General Assembly for three-year terms in groups
of six each year. This is the general committee of the Assembly to promote higher standards of living, better health,
respect for human rights, and international cooperation in
education and the arts.

ECOSOC has created many commissions and committees to study and report on various subjects ranging from
the economic condition of Europe to the international
opium trade. It is the UN body that makes agreements
with the specialized agencies, such as the Food and Agriculture Organization (FAO) or the Universal Postal Union
(UPU), subject to the approval of the General Assembly.

ECOSOC is also authorized to recognize nongovernmental organizations having technical knowledge that may
help it in its work. More than thirteen hundred such organizations have been given what is called "consultative
status." They are permitted to send observers to public

meetings of the Council and its commissions. They may also speak at such meetings and present written statements which will be circulated as documents of these bodies.

The consulting organizations include, for example, the International Chamber of Commerce, International Confederation of Free Trade Unions, International Association of Juvenile Court Judges, Rotary International, Salvation Army, and International Islamic Economic Organization.

ECOSOC reports regularly to the General Assembly and often brings forward questions upon which the Assembly may wish to pass resolutions.

The other main UN organs are the Trusteeship Council, described in Chapter 6, and the International Court of Justice, described in Chapter 7.

The Secretary-General

The Secretary-General is the chief administrative officer of the United Nations, and he also has important political responsibilities.

The Secretary-General is "appointed by the General Assembly upon the recommendation of the Security Council." This means that before being voted upon by the General Assembly, the name of a proposed Secretary-General must be approved by the Council subject to the veto of any one of the five permanent members. This requirement enhances the importance of the Secretary-General, for he has been accepted by all the Great Powers, at least at the time of his election. He is therefore in a position to stand above the conflict and to mediate in times of severe tension.

The Charter gives the Secretary-General the privilege of coming before the Security Council to present for its consideration any matter that in his opinion may threaten the peace. The first Secretary-General, Trygve Lie, developed this privilege to include direct mediation among delegates to bring reconciliation of conflicts, when no other person was in a position to take the initiative. As his successor said in 1957: "I believe . . . that the Secretary-General should . . . help in filling any vacuum that may appear in the systems which the Charter and traditional diplomacy provide for the safeguarding of peace and security."

Trygve Lie of Norway was appointed Secretary-General

on February 1, 1946, for five years. In 1950, when the Security Council was unable to agree on a recommendation regarding his successor, he was continued in office for a further three years. After two years, however, he resigned, and Dag Hammarskjöld of Sweden was appointed for a term of five years. Mr. Hammarskjöld was sworn into office on April 10, 1953. In September, 1957, he was reappointed for a further five-year term. On his death in 1961 in a plane crash he was succeeded by U Thant of Burma.

Every year the Secretary-General makes a report to the General Assembly on the work of the Organization. He also acts as administrative officer for the meetings of the Assembly, the Security Council, the Trusteeship Council, and ECOSOC. In these jobs he employs various members of the Secretariat, of which he is the executive head.

The Secretariat

In the UN headquarters in New York is a staff of over three thousand people working directly under the Secretary-General. There are other headquarters, in Geneva, Bangkok, The Hague, Montreal, Santiago de Chile, and so on, where specialized agencies or branches of the UN have other hundreds of employees.

There is no place in the world where people from so many different nations work in the same organization as at the UN in New York. UN employees come to the Secretariat from nearly every country on earth, including some countries that do not belong to the UN. But they do not represent their countries. According to Article 100 of the Charter, the Secretary-General and the staff shall not seek or receive instructions from any other authority external to the Organization. Moreover, each member undertakes not to seek to influence its own nationals who are on the staff.

The delegates to the Assembly represent their countries and get instructions from home; their countrymen on the staff do not.

How about the betrayal of secrets? There are no secrets that involve the security of a country. Tourists are not allowed loose in the Secretariat office building because they would interfere with the work; but the information in the building is open to delegates from all countries.

The principle of international loyalty emphasized in the Charter would have been abandoned if the 1960 Soviet proposal for a three-man board, or "troika" to replace the office of Secretary-General had been adopted. The Soviets had proposed that one member should represent the Western Allies, one the communist bloc, and one the neutrals, and that each member should have a veto; this would have meant that each member would receive instructions from an authority external to the Organization. In the opinion of most of the member nations, a most important quality of the Secretariat would have been destroyed. They therefore rejected the proposal.

The UN buildings contain nearly all the equipment and services that the Organization needs. There is even a fire department to take care of small fires, though in case of a serious fire the New York City Fire Department would come to help. There are restaurants, a bank, a library, and a post office, though the delegates and staff have to find lodgings outside.

There is an international school in New York for the children of UN delegates and staff. In May of 1960 it had about 330 children from 47 countries, and 34 teachers from 14 different countries, most of them speaking two or more languages.

The UN post office is operated by the United States Post Office, but the UN Postal Administration, a part of the Secretariat, issues its own stamps, valid on mail posted at Headquarters to any part of the world.

The staff has an elaborate job to do in managing the meetings in the New York headquarters. The topics to be discussed must be examined and the necessary background material made ready for delegates to use when they need it. All the necessary interpreters have to be on hand to translate all the languages that the delegates at any meeting will speak. Stenographers record the proceedings in English, French, Spanish, Chinese, and Russian. The speeches are also piped to a recording room where they are permanently recorded.

The "simultaneous interpreters" sit in soundproof

booths overlooking the meeting, listening to the speaker and translating at the same time. Thus the dials at every seat can be turned to give the proceedings in English, French, Spanish, Chinese, or Russian by setting the dial. In the meetings of the Security Council and the Disarmament Commission two "consecutive interpreters" also listen to the speaker. When he has finished they repeat the whole speech, with appropriate emphasis and gestures, in English and in French, if he has spoken in any other language.

The United Nations *Journal* prints summaries of the days' meetings in English and French. It is printed during the night to be available the next day.

The Department of Public Information publishes books, pamphlets, and magazines describing the work of the UN; it directs the Headquarters bookstore, and has sales outlets all over the world. It has shown documentary films in over ninety countries, with sound tracks in more than thirty languages. The DPI issues press releases, but these are not exclusive; it gives every facility to newsmen to write their own dispatches from "United Nations, N.Y."

Radio news broadcasts by the UN staff go out in some thirty languages for all regions of the world, telling what happened during the day. The UN reporters do not "slant" the news to favor any side of an argument, so their reports are well received all over the world.

The records of the UN proceedings are preserved in a file room with special protection against fire. There are also more than three thousand treaties contained in safes, for under the Charter all treaties must be registered with the UN and published by it. If a treaty is not registered, no UN organ will recognize it as binding.

The UN headquarters staff does a considerable amount of scientific and statistical work that is not covered by any of the agency staffs in other parts of the world. The New York staff has made studies, for instance, of the rights of women, the newest methods of house construction, the growth of national populations, and a proposal for a set of standard road signs that can be understood without words. It issues important studies and reference books on economic and social development, such as the *World Economic Survey, Statistical Yearbook, Demographic*

Yearbook, International Trade Statistics, and *Report on World Social Situation.* The staff collects information for all the UN organs and agencies. It also handles the expenses and draws up the budget for the Secretary-General to present to the Assembly.

About a million tourists visit the New York Headquarters every year. Guides are provided to show groups of tourists around. You can be admitted to the galleries of the meeting halls as long as there are vacant seats.

The guards will not allow you to make a speech from the galleries. They do not have the right to arrest people, but they can put disorderly tourists out into New York, U.S.A.

Costs of the UN

The UN, being an organization that deals mainly in moral force and the exchange of knowledge, costs almost nothing in comparison with international enterprises that have to meet material needs. For the regular UN budget of about $100,000,000, the United States contributes the equivalent of about 15 cents per head of its population; some other nations, with smaller contributions, pay more per head.

For comparison, the original Marshall Plan was estimated to cost 24,000 million dollars, or 240 times the UN yearly budget. Of the various special programs, in 1959, UNICEF used nearly $27,000,000, UNRWA $38,000,000 for care of Arab refugees, and the Expanded Program of Technical Assistance over $31,000,000.

These funds are raised by special contributions from governments and private givers, and are not paid directly by the UN. All the specialized agencies have their own membership, which may differ from that of the UN, and assess their own dues, getting no subsidies from other UN funds except the Technical Assistance Fund and the Special Fund.

The UN activities that are agreed by the members to be essential for protecting and building the peace are rapidly rising in cost, and the small budgets of the Organization and its affiliated agencies need to be steadily increased. The amounts needed are small compared with the national budgets of the members, but there are always political obstacles to such appropriations, which can be overcome only by wide and hearty public support.

The biggest costs of international action are, of course, the costs of armament. In this setting it is evident that if the UN could profitably use twice as much money, the members could afford to supply it with no noticeable effect on their finances.

The financing of peace-keeping operations has become a serious problem because of the refusal of the communist countries, and of France and some others, to pay their assessments for the operations in the Congo and in Palestine. The Soviet Union's refusal is the most serious, especially in its interpretation of the Charter responsibilities of the Security Council and the General Assembly.

Peace-keeping forces, invited into a country by its own government in order to help it keep order, are not the same as UN military forces making war against an aggressor, as was the case in Korea. Thus the UNEF in Palestine was invited by Egypt and by the other warring nations involved in the Suez affair: France, Britain, and Israel. Since the force was not fighting anyone, its use could be decided upon by the Assembly and charged against the UN budget. The UN army in Korea, on the other hand, was ordered by the Security Council, as required by the Charter—the Soviet Union being absent at the time. The Assembly could apportion the costs of the Korean War, according to Article 17 of the Charter, but this point did not arise because the expenses were paid by the nations that sent forces, chiefly the United States.

The Congo operation, like that in Palestine, could have been decided upon by the Assembly, since it was not a war; but in fact it was ordered by the Security Council, the Soviet Union voting in favor. The Assembly allocated the costs, as required by Article 17, but the Soviets claimed that the decision on costs should have been left to the Security Council, and on these grounds of illegality they refused to pay.

The World Court gave an advisory opinion that the Congo operation was a UN expense and chargeable to the members, but the Soviets denied the legality of the decision.

In 1964, as the time for the 19th General Assembly session approached, the situation became critical. Article 19 of the Charter provides that any member that is two years in arrears in its apportioned dues shall lose its vote in the Assembly unless the Assembly votes that it is unable to pay. The chief Soviet delegate stated on April 17 that the Soviet Union denied the legality of the assessments and would not pay, and that if it were deprived of its vote the UN would be broken up.

Further negotiations between the United States and the Soviet Union were reported to be in progress. If the relations between the Soviet Union and the West should continue to improve, it was suggested that a revival of the effective powers of the Security Council might help to solve the financial crisis.

Amending the Charter

The Charter provided that the Assembly and Security Council must consider in 1955 whether to hold a special Convention for amending the Charter. This is one of the two ways in which amendments can be submitted to the members. The other is for the Assembly to approve an amendment by a vote of two-thirds of the membership.

But in any case a proposed amendment must go to the members for ratification and cannot come into force until it is ratified by two-thirds of the members including the Big Five. That is, the veto may stand in the way of final ratification.

But the Charter, though hard to amend by formal voting, is flexible, like the Constitution of the United States. Just as the people of the United States have quietly mummified the Electoral College and have built up the political parties, not mentioned in the Constitution, so the UN, finding the Security Council often unable to act, has been shifting its duties to other organs not paralyzed by any veto power.

The most important informal changes from the original UN, as conceived at San Francisco, include the following:

The UN armed forces, provided in Article 43, have practically been dropped. (The UN operations in Egypt and the Congo are quite different.) Articles 44 to 48, giving details of how the UN forces shall be used, are dead, at least for the present. Article 106, authorizing the Big Five to act as a temporary Security Council, never has come alive because of the quick-growing disagreements among the Big Five. Article 23 provides that the Assembly shall elect the temporary members of the Security Council with due regard to their contributions to peace. This requirement turned out not to be practical.

On the positive side, several additions have been made to the original Charter. One was the agreement in the Security Council that when a permanent member fails to vote, that is not a veto. The Assembly has repeatedly pressed the Council to classify more topics as not subject to veto.

The increased influence of the Secretary-General has made this office more important than originally conceived. Another change is the Assembly's insistence on discussing the treatment of dependent territories, a subject not positively allowed by the language of the Charter except in the Trusteeships.

The Uniting for Peace resolutions drastically changed the relationships originally intended to be established by the Charter between the Security Council and the Assembly.

Article 2-(7), which forbids the UN to intervene in matters that are within the domestic jurisdiction of a member state, was of course impossible to maintain, since it contradicts other features of the Charter, especially those concerning non-self-governing territories and human rights. The Organization has overcome this prohibition by the device of calling an internal condition, such as the apartheid policies of South Africa, a threat to international peace and security.

Another example of how the UN is able to meet an unforeseen responsibility is the way it took over the problem of the Italian colonies. It was strictly the right of the conquering powers—Britain, France, the United States, and the U.S.S.R.—to settle the future of Libya, Somaliland, and Eritrea. After three years of negotiating and inability to agree, the four Powers agreed to let the Assembly decide. There have been clear signs of a demand that the UN take sovereignty over various wild areas, including the sea bottom, the South Polar Continent, and outer space.

In general, however, the Assembly may only make recommendations, and the nations concerned will afterward decide whether to accept them or not.

A number of supplementary agreements among various member states have spelled out some details not covered in the Charter but consistent with it. One is the treaty with the United States defining the legal position of the Headquarters district in New York. Most important are the regional treaties supplementing UN efforts to keep the peace, such as the North Atlantic Treaty and the Organization of American States. There is also a Convention on Privileges and Immunities, defining the rights of UN officials, property, funds, and communications.

There is within the UN a strong resistance to formal amendment of the Charter, and since 1955 the calling of a special Convention has been repeatedly postponed. At the same time, the Organization is able to change its ways of operating to meet unforeseen dangers and problems.

In 1963 the Assembly adopted by a large majority a resolution proposing an amendment to the Charter that would enlarge the Security Council from eleven to fifteen members and ECOSOC from eighteen to twenty-seven members. The purpose was to make room for more representation on these two bodies for the new Asian and African members.

Everyone expressed general agreement that these amendments would be desirable, but the Soviet delegate announced that his government had been informed by Communist China that before any amendments were passed it must be given China's permanent seat on the Council. Since the ratification of a Charter amendment requires the consent of all the permanent members of the Council, the Soviet Union, on behalf of the absent Chinese member, would not ratify the amendment. Meanwhile it recommended redistribution of the seats to give fair representation to Asia and Africa. This action amounted to notice that the Soviet Union would permit no changes in the Charter until Communist China is given China's seat.

THE PHILOSOPHY
OF THE UNITED NATIONS

The Rockefeller Panel Report on U.S. Foreign Policy, in 1959, declared:

"The UN stands, finally, as a symbol of the world order that will be built. . . . To measure the UN's contribution, one need only ask how much meaner and poorer, how much less touched by hope or reason, would be the world scene if it suddenly ceased to exist."

When the victorious nations met at San Francisco in 1945 to organize for peace there was one choice that had already been made—they had chosen to set up a world-wide organization, a new and better organized League of Nations. Everyone knew that there were serious differences among the nations on various questions. If the nations were going to set up a worldwide organization, its charter would have to be loose enough to tolerate nations with deeply antagonistic views. On the other hand, if they had intended to found a true federal government with full power to enforce its laws against any rebellious state, then the UN would have to be composed entirely of nations that were agreed on the most controversial issues. In other words, the UN could have had a stronger charter, if only one class of nations, such as the "Western world," or the Americas, had been in it. Such a like-minded combination might have been able to do without the veto, as the Organization of American States has done. But it would not have been any kind of a world organization.

The decision to hold the San Francisco meeting was a

decision to create a world organization that would include all the hostile camps that might be destined to take form. However much division might come into the world—over communism, or colonialism, or race and religious conflicts, or the difference between rich and poor countries—so long as the UN goes on there would be a place where the contending parties could argue in the presence of others who are more concerned for peace than they are for the victory of either side. Such a relationship might not prevent the fatal World War III, but in the opinion of the statesmen of all parties, such an organized arguing place is the best hope of preventing it.

With that belief in the desperate necessity of having a worldwide United Nations, the delegates at San Francisco created "as strong an organization as all of them could agree upon and as, in their judgment, could, in practice, be effective at this stage in the history of the world." These are the words of Trygve Lie, the first Secretary-General of the UN.

The Charter binds all the members, including the Great Powers, to work for peace and not to use or threaten force on their own account against any nation. It binds the members to help the UN in suppressing aggression and to give no help to the aggressors. If all the Great Powers would faithfully keep these promises there would be no world war, even if some small nation might occasionally have to be reduced to order. But if one of the Great Powers should break the peace and if others should decide to resist by force, no possible world organization could suppress the Powers on either side of such a conflict.

What a world organization can do, and what it is doing fairly well, is to lead the Great Powers to look before they leap. If the small nations do not like what the Powers are doing, they can say so and the Powers feel called upon to answer. While they argue, it is possible that crisis after crisis can come and go without quite heating up to the explosion point. If the UN is to act as a forum for arguing among hostile nations, it cannot use force against any nation that is big enough to blow up the forum itself. This is the reason that the United States insisted on the "veto," and that the other Great Powers joined in demanding it as a condition of signing the Charter.

The Veto

The veto embodied in the Charter prevents the Security Council from using force against anyone except by a vote of seven out of the eleven members, including the "concurring votes" of all of the five permanent members.

The veto is a recognition of the fact that the limit of the UN's power to use its own police force is a limit short of world war. If the disagreements among the Great Powers should ever reach the point where one of these Powers must be disciplined by military action, the UN would no longer be in the picture, and the fatal third war would already be beyond hope of remedy. The veto is a safeguard against fatally big ideas in the UN itself—big ideas of enforcing peace in a situation where no human agency could enforce it. The UN is warned that its job of keeping the peace does not include any kind of disciplinary action that would bring on the world war.

The police powers of the Security Council, therefore, cannot be used in such a way as to corner one of the Great Powers and force it to fight. The veto is a built-in protection against UN action that would surely start a new world war.

Experience has shown that the Assembly, in which there is no veto, can "act" in cases where the Security Council must not "act," simply because the Assembly's action is purely moral and advisory. World opinion is a strong force, but it does not kill soldiers or civilians, and therefore does not have to be answered by a shooting war.

It is true that in several ways the UN as a peacemaker has not worked out as the San Francisco Conference expected. On the minus side there were two serious disappointments: the failure to settle World War II; and the excessive use of the veto.

Remains of World War II

One disappointment is that the peace treaties to end World War II did not come through quickly. It was expected that the victorious Powers would impose peace on the defeated Axis and the UN could start from there. But as it has worked out, the Powers have not been able to agree on peace terms for the principal Axis countries. Treaties were signed only with the East European allies of Germany that came under Soviet control, and these treaties have been a bone of contention between the Western Powers and the Soviet Union.

The years went by and the Powers could not agree on treaties for Japan or Germany. In Japan there were no Soviet troops, and so the Western Powers could make their own peace with that country, leaving it still at war with the U.S.S.R. (Later the Soviet Union also made peace with Japan and that country was admitted to the UN.) In Germany part of the country is under Soviet control, and that control cannot be lifted except by a peace in which the Soviet Government will join. The Western Powers have made as much peace as they can with the part of Germany not controlled by the Soviets. The Germans find it a poor substitute for freedom and reunion.

These stubborn remains of World War II create problems that threaten world peace—problems such as the Berlin blockade and the disputes about how to unify Germany. These problems concern the UN, although in theory it was not intended that the UN should take an interest in the defeated countries until peace had been signed. The UN Assembly does not hesitate to urge the Powers to hasten the final peace treaties. In time its constant moral pressure may be the force that overcomes the last obstacles to the final ending of the war.

Too Many Vetoes

The second disappointment in the peace machinery has been the frequent use of the veto by the Soviet representative in the Security Council. At San Francisco, the Great Powers all agreed in insisting on the right of veto. They went further. They also agreed that the right of veto in the Council should apply to everything except procedural questions. The theory advanced by the Great Powers in support of such sweeping rights of veto was that once the Security Council takes jurisdiction over any international dispute and begins taking action, even in an effort to reach a peaceful settlement, a chain of events is set in motion that may end with military enforcement action. They made one exception. This was the proviso that if one of them were a party to a dispute, it must abstain from voting on the proceedings of the Council in its efforts to reach a peaceful settlement through mediation and negotiation.

The veto in this form was accepted with a good deal of reluctance by the smaller countries. Unfortunately there are many cases where the veto can be used that do not fit the arguments for it that were advanced at San Francisco. For example, most of the vetoes cast by the Soviet Union in the early years were against the admission of various countries to membership in the United Nations. In some other decisions, the Soviet delegate has voted "No" to a proposal that happened not to conform to the Soviet line of policy.

On the other hand, the Soviet veto of various disarmament proposals, although it has been distressing to the other members, is not necessarily an abuse of the veto power. Any disarmament treaty, to be effective, must be willingly and loyally accepted by all the Great Powers. If the terms of a proposed treaty are not acceptable to any Power, it can of course prevent that treaty by merely refusing to sign. The veto, therefore, is no more than notification of the plain fact that the proposals are not unanimously accepted. This may be an unpleasant fact, but the veto is not what makes it so.

In the Assembly the smaller nations, who naturally resent the veto power, have a majority of the votes, and the Assembly has voted from time to time to admonish the Powers about their use of the veto. It is hard to see how anything more effective for changing the use of the veto could be found. There is no force on earth capable of making a Power give up what it regards as its legal rights, unless it may be the force of world opinion.

There are, of course, many people who would like to see the Charter amended so as to restrict or abolish the veto power. The Charter cannot be amended according to its own terms except with the concurrence of the Big Five —that is, any amendment can be vetoed. This also has reason, for if the smaller nations could unite to change the Charter over the objections of any Great Power, that Power would be likely to resign, and for practical purposes there would be no United Nations. Here, also, the veto

represents the unpleasant difference between the real world
and a much more orderly but imaginary one.

Propaganda

Once the fundamental decision was taken to set up a
worldwide organization, another unpleasant consequence
necessarily followed. In the UN there has to be free speech.
Everyone who belongs has a right to say whatever he
wants to say, right or wrong, honest or dishonest. That is,
the UN can be used by adversaries as a platform for their
propaganda. Their opponents sometimes feel that if only
they could be thrown out how it would clear the air! No
more big lies, no more campaigns of hate and vilification.
Peace and quiet would settle over the Council and the
Assembly. But it would be the same kind of peace and
quiet that we find in the inner councils of a nation at war,
where the enemies are outside and only friends are inside.

It is not a black mark against the United Nations that in
its halls the most flimsy arguments and the most subtle
deceptions can be laid before the meeting and solemnly
put into the official record. This is one of the principal
advantages of the UN. If there is any nation in the world
that is putting out dishonest propaganda, the place where
that propaganda is most likely to be poisonous is in private
arguments, among ignorant or ill-balanced people. It has
little chance of deceiving UN delegates, who have heard
all sides many times over.

On the contrary, in the UN, if there is any dishonest
propaganda afloat, the author of it must bring it in under
the withering inspection of men of all nations and religions,
including his own allies. Or if he tries to hide anything,
his opponents will drag it in. The fearful heat of world
moral judgment is proved by the desperate efforts of those
who are in the wrong to defend themselves by arguments
that they hope will cover them.

No Great Power would dare to state its sovereign will in
the United Nations Assembly and then sit tight and wait
for the lesser nations to cringe before it. No matter how
arrogant a Power may be in its actions, it has to talk. The
smaller nations do not cringe. They rise and say what
they think.

So long as men can do wrong and tell lies, one of the greatest values of a marketplace of opinion is that such men are on view in the market. In the long run, open disagreements openly arrived at are more likely to be settled according to the moral judgment of mankind than secret plottings covered by a veil of silence.

World Government?

The question is often raised whether the UN is a sort of baby world government that in time will grow up to rule the nations with a world system of law, a world police, and a world income tax. Those who are impatient to see a world government criticize the UN for failing to be one or to show signs of growing into one.

Those who fear the thought of a world government criticize the UN for being the entering camel's head in the door of the tent that in time will be followed by the whole beast.

Any positive statement on this question has to be hedged around with qualifications, because the meanings of the necessary words can be easily misinterpreted. What, for instance, is a government? If you consider a city government, a provincial or state government, and a national government, they are plainly not the same thing, especially in their relation to that final authority called "sovereignty." In the United States, for instance, the final authority to use force against the citizen—that is, the police power—rests in some cases with the state and in others with the federal government. It is not a simple matter to picture what a world government would be like if there were to be one.

Another fact that needs to be considered is that in the long run all governments that are freely set up by the people "depend on the consent of the governed." The UN was not designed to pave the way for any dictator to conquer the world. If any world government should grow up under the benevolent auspices of the UN, it would depend on the consent of the people of the world. So far as anyone can see now, the people of the world are not prepared to give the UN or any other authority enough powers to add up to a recognizable federal government of the world.

During the Suez and Hungarian crises of 1956–57 there

was some criticism of the UN on the ground that it had a "double standard" of judgment, since it procured the withdrawal of the Israeli, French, and British troops from Egypt but did not get the Soviet troops out of Hungary. This criticism may have been based upon an unspoken and perhaps unconscious assumption that the UN ought to act like a world government—judging the nations under world law and forcing them to obey the law. That is not what the UN is for, and the people of the world have given it no such authority.

The UN applied a single standard of moral judgment in its request and recommendations on the Suez situation and on Hungary. It expressed the moral judgment of the majority of the nations, but it had not been given the legal right or the power to force anyone to obey. The Soviet Government refused to comply with the UN requests, and the only penalty was the condemnation expressed in the Report on Hungary as accepted by the Assembly.

The fact that the UN is not authorized to make war on the Soviet Union in Hungary's behalf reflects, as the Secretary-General declared in his annual report, "the profound will of the peoples of the world to avoid general war." It is much easier for private persons to call for "enforcement" of what they are sure is right than for the responsible leaders of the nations to find a path through the minefields of the world with some hope of avoiding total disaster.

The peoples of the world are not prepared to give any central world authority the final sovereign powers that characterize a federal nation like the United States—such as the final power to tax the citizen, to punish citizens for crimes, to draft them for the army, and to control the rules of trade regardless of the desires of the member states. In general, they are not ready to let any central legislature make international law without the consent of the nations.

If the world's peoples should ever be ready for such a federal government, it would be when they have decided that the conflicts among peoples, classes, races, and religions are no harder to compromise than they are in a federal government such as the United States. That will be a long time, if ever.

But there are some parts of the relations among sovereign states that can be administered by a world authority with the consent of each nation that accepts the authority. For instance, everyone recognizes that the mails must be carried between countries under rules established for the world. The Universal Postal Union was the first world authority to be set up, and all civilized nations have to belong to it. Equally good reasons have led to the creation of the other specialized agencies governing the relations of their members along certain lines of action.

These organizations are voluntary arrangements, and are not imposed on unwilling countries by any supergovernment. The nations organize certain activities in order to prevent confusion and prohibitive costs of doing business. The specialized agencies are useful in themselves and they also are useful in bringing even unfriendly nations to sit together for a practical purpose.

The same general principle applies to international law, as it is called. The United Nations cannot pass an international law binding on any nation without its specific assent, except in the rare case where the Security Council, with all the permanent members consenting, can order a pair of smaller nations to stop fighting and start talking. The Assembly can pass a resolution advising the nations what to do, but if the nations refuse, the only punishment is a resolution of the Assembly condemning their refusal. This moral power is a strong power but it is not law.

The UN can cause international law to be created by the free consent of the nations in at least two ways.

The Conventions that the UN offers to the nations become international law for all the nations that ratify them. A treaty is a piece of international law, enforced not by any international police but by the moral penalties of dishonor that fall on treaty-breakers. The day of 100 percent obedience to international law by all the nations may be as far off as the day when all men honor their personal promises, but there is nevertheless a moral penalty for broken faith that is not to be despised.

In another way the United Nations can be said to sponsor the making of law. In the International Court of Justice, those nations that voluntarily submit themselves to the Court can be judged like the citizens of any sovereign state. If a nation is accused by another nation or by the UN of violating its treaty obligations, the Court may judge not only the facts but the interpretation of the treaty, and its interpretation will then be the law.

Is this then the subtle beginning of a world government that will take away the sovereignty of the free nations? The question sounds ominous, but in fact it has no immediate meaning. What instruments of agreement the nations freely decide to adopt among themselves are surely within the sovereign power of each nation that chooses to join. The moral obligation to honor promises freely made is no tyranny. If the obligation of honor is imposed by any Power higher than the nations, that Authority is not one that God-fearing men dare resent. And back of that moral Authority is the hard fact that peaceful agreement and co-operation are a way of life in a world where the Last Judgment is more than likely to happen soon, and a way of life is desperately wanted.

Who Can Belong?

The question of admitting new members to the United Nations is not so much a legal matter of interpretation of the Charter as a question of what sort of institution the United Nations is intended to be.

When the Charter was written in 1945, the obligation of the members to work sincerely for peace was emphasized. Surely all peoples want peace, and all nations worthy of membership in the new league for peace must be peace-loving. The defeated Axis Powers, of course, were to be suitably reeducated and purified, until they too became peace-loving and fit to join with the decent nations. Everyone knew there would be quarrels, but it seemed reasonable to say in Article 4 of the Charter that membership is open to all other "peace-loving" states if they accept the obligations of the Charter and in the judgment of the Organization are able and willing to carry out these obligations.

Before the Charter was signed a question arose about the Ukraine and Byelorussia, which to the rest of the world appeared to be not free states able to accept any obligations to the UN but mere provinces of the Soviet

Union subject to the federal government in Moscow. To the Soviet delegates, on the other hand, it seemed plain enough that Canada, Australia, and the other Dominions would be under the orders of the British Government, and that all the Latin American states were mere satellites of the United States that would have to vote as ordered by Washington. These suppositions may not have all been true, but they had to be taken into account, and so the original members included some that in the judgment of most of the Organization were hardly "able and willing" to carry out the obligations of free Charter members.

During the first ten years, however, only nine additional countries were added to the original fifty-one Charter members. No state can be admitted without the "recommendation" of the Security Council. The Soviet delegate vetoed all applicants that were in any way objectionable to his country, such as the Republic of Korea, Libya, Italy, and Japan. The majority of the Council turned down all those that it regarded as under Soviet control, such as Hungary, Romania, and Bulgaria.

In 1946 the United States suggested a compromise by which the candidates of both factions would be admitted, but the Soviets refused. Later the Soviets wanted a "package deal," and the Western nations refused. Finally in 1955 it was arranged, and sixteen nations were admitted at one time. Later additions brought the total membership to 113 in 1964. Still excluded by Soviet objections were West Germany, South Vietnam, and the ROK, and by Western objections North Vietnam, North Korea, and East Germany.

There is wide agreement that in the long run the UN ought to include all the independent nations of the world. But how many shortcomings to overlook for the sake of universal membership will long be a matter of dispute. In view of the fact that most nations have some faults in their UN behavior, and that no nation however proudly sovereign is absolutely independent, the arguments are bound to contain much cloudy judgment about where to draw the line. There is, however, no doubt that the central philosophy of the UN, accepted by all the members, includes the belief that some day its membership should include every nation on earth.

The problem of China has troubled the United Nations ever since 1949, when the Chinese Nationalist Government of Chiang Kai-shek was driven off the mainland and took refuge on the island of Taiwan (Formosa). It was replaced on the mainland by a communist government called the People's Republic of China. The UN Assembly has repeatedly refused the demands of communist members that it receive delegates from the People's Republic in place of those from Taiwan.

The problem is complicated by the fact that under the Charter, Nationalist China is one of the Big Five—a permanent member of the Security Council, with a veto.

The communist position is that to seat the delegation from Communist China would not require an amendment to the Charter but merely a "procedural" decision in the Assembly (by simple majority vote) that this delegation is the rightful representative of China, with a permanent membership on the Council. The Assembly has, however, decided that the question is an "important" one and that such a replacement of one China by the other requires a two-thirds vote.

In 1963 the resolution "for the Restoration of the lawful rights of the People's Republic" received 42 votes, with 57 against and 12 abstentions. In 1961 the vote had been 42 in favor, 56 against, and 12 abstentions.

The division is a mixed one. In favor are not only all the communist states, but also the United Kingdom and the Scandinavian countries. Opposed are not only the United States and Canada, but most of Europe, all of Latin America except Cuba, and most of Africa.

A logical solution would be to give Nationalist China, which has become a small nation, an ordinary seat in the UN; and to give Communist China, with 650 million people, the Big Power seat reserved for "China" in the Charter. Neither the communists nor the Nationalists, however, will admit that there are two Chinas, although there plainly are two. Each claims to be the only China, and denies the other's right to exist.

The moral arguments against Communist China are strong but useless. It has made war on the UN in Korea, and is still at war, since all we have there is a fragile truce. It has treated the test-ban treaty with contempt. It has recently invaded India, and is interfering in Southeast Asia—in Laos and in Vietnam, for instance. It promotes war in Africa. It is clearly not "peace-loving" nor willing to carry out the obligations of the Charter.

Yet it would be absurd to look closely at the qualifications for membership set forth in the Charter. Much of the Organization's business is caused by the aggressive operations of some members who are already in and cannot be put out. The UN has turned out to be not a club of gentle souls but a community of good and bad members, which is something quite different.

In the long run, if the UN survives, all nations will have to belong, however violent their habits may be. But how long the run is not easily foreseen.

One Member, One Vote

The General Assembly of the United Nations, where every member state has one vote, is analogous to the Senate of the United States, in which the states, large and small, have an equal voice. Is this democratic?

The democracy of the United Nations, like that of the United States, is affected by the peculiarity of having to take account of the rights of large and small states as well as of the rights of people. The UN is in the main a democracy of nations, not of individual human beings. In a rough way there is a touch of popular democracy in the Security Council, where the veto gives the biggest nations—at least in a military sense as of 1945—a bigger voice than the smaller ones. There have been proposals that the Charter should be amended to "weight" the votes of the members in the Assembly according to their population, but it is not clear how to draw an acceptable amendment.

In the Assembly, where most of the vitality of the UN has become concentrated, Costa Rica and Lebanon have as many votes as the United Kingdom and the United States. This is not democratic in the sense of giving every human being equal voting weight in the Assembly.

If the Assembly were a legislature with power to make laws binding on the nations, the strong would of course not consent to be members, any more than the big states of the United States would consent to be governed by the U.S. Senate alone, without the balancing force of the House of Representatives, where they are represented in proportion to their population. But the UN General Assembly was not set up to make world law. It is an organ set up to discuss world affairs and express as nearly as possible the moral judgments of the world. Voting is a part of this expression but not the chief part. The moral force in the Assembly, by which it can hurt a nation that is doing wrong and help one that is doing right, depends in the last analysis not only on the final vote but even more on what was said, who said it, and what the people of the world think of the arguments put forward and of the parts played by the nations concerned.

Necessarily a strong nation has a greater weight in the arguments than its one vote would seem to indicate, since its actions and intentions are of greater weight in the making of world events. Moreover it is evident that in the UN the members often vote in groups, either following a strong nation that represents the position they favor, or uniting behind some regional or political interest that they have in common. These groupings and evidences of leadership are not uniform, except almost always in the Soviet bloc; they normally shift according to the question at issue. In fact, the moral effect of the Assembly's action depends partly on what groupings have been shown in the voting and in the discussion.

With the addition of numerous Asian and African states since 1954, there has been some uneasiness lest an "Afro-Asian bloc" should take to voting against the West because of resentments brought down from the heyday of colonialism. Apparently, however, when the Western nations are surely right they will draw strong support in Asia and Africa; on a more doubtful question they will find the vote divided.

It should be clear that there is more in making and applying the judgment of mankind than can be registered by giving either every nation or every individual an equal vote. It may also be worth noting that for the making of peace, the moral position of the small nations is on the face of it better than that of the Great Powers. No one can wreck the world except some Great Power. No little nation, however belligerent, can start a world war if the

Great Powers refuse to join. The responsibility for peace therefore rests entirely on the strongest nations, and the pure desire not to be destroyed in other people's quarrels rests in its most undiluted form among the small nations.

It is more than a mere accident that in the United Nations, where men from all sorts of countries meet to discuss human affairs, the small countries so often contribute statesmen of a much greater relative importance than the size of their country. Great men can occur anywhere, in a big or a little country, but they cannot be seen in their full size except on a world stage. The UN provides that stage, and so brings to the help of hard-pressed humanity men who would otherwise have little chance to become known.

On the other hand, there will inevitably be a limit to the admission of extremely small islands or other communities that in the exercise of self-determination have voted to be independent rather than to join some larger nation. The limits will be fixed by a realization of the fact that a few hundred people cannot be allowed to claim a vote in the UN merely by calling themselves a "nation," and this limitation will presumably be imposed by the members deciding that the applicant is not "able to carry out the obligations" of membership.

The Great Revolutions

The United Nations is not the cause of the great revolutions that are going on at present, though it may well be the ship that will carry the human race alive through the troubled waters. The world is going through at least three different waves of progress at the same time. There have also been waves of backwash toward savagery.

The oldest wave of progress is the anticolonial revolution, now nearing its end. The vast majority of the peoples who came under foreign domination in the four hundred years after the discovery of America are now independent nations, and nearly all the rest are being groomed for independence. The fact that India, Pakistan, and the new African states are members of the UN does much to give their new governments confidence and dignity, abroad and at home.

The disturbances caused by the anticolonial revolution have not yet calmed down. There are still resentments among those who were recently under foreign rule, as well as among the peoples who have not yet become self-governing. These resentments become evident in the UN disputes over the treatment of dependent territories.

The next oldest world revolution is the outburst of scientific knowledge and invention that began seriously to transform human society in the Western world during the nineteenth century. This revolution has opened a magical world of rapidly expanding production. There are limits to this expansion, but they are not easily understood by millions of hungry people who never before had any hope of escape from lifelong misery. The knowledge of the magic of science has called forth an insistent demand for a share in this magic. The strains that come from impatience cannot be avoided. Impatient people may grasp at false promises and be led into new slavery in search of the bright vision of enough to eat.

The dark sides of the scientific revolution are also to be taken into account. Science has almost no moral principles. It will serve a Hitler almost as well as it will serve a free democracy, enough to create terrible dangers. And science has given us the atom and a hilltop view of the end of the world.

Another aspect of scientific progress is that science will not only serve fairly well an intelligent dictator; it will also undermine any government that is unduly influenced by a stupid and corrupt ruling class. Factories can be built in such a country, and enough progress can be made to stimulate the expectations of the people. But if the government is too weak to collect heavy income taxes or to reform an oppressive landholding system, business and industry cannot prosper. Such countries are frequently in danger of revolution and dictatorship. A dictator can at least promise to "make the trains run on time." But thereafter may follow political tyranny and new miseries.

Technical assistance to countries of all sorts will produce results of different kinds. In the long run it is a hard fact that successful use of science to raise the standard of living depends on honest and intelligent management both of industry and of politics. While some nations go on to illustrate this hard fact by racking internal disorders, it is well to have the UN holding up a moral standard for mankind. And that brings us to the third revolution that is sweeping the world.

The third revolution is closely related to the other two. It is the growing demand of oppressed peoples for justice and for democracy in government. In past ages millions of human beings took what came and never dreamed of any escape from whatever masters fate had set over them. That is not so true today. The change from foreign rule to independence has taught men that their foreign masters were not permanent. They think that perhaps their home-grown landlords and moneylenders may also be subject to overthrow. And the coming of the scientific revolution has forced the process of education. People who never before knew of any life beyond their village are learning to read and are listening to the radio in the village square. Those who sat in darkness are beginning to see a light, and they will not be quiet. In their own lives are unhappy experiences that they have long resented without hope of escape. Now they have names for wrongs, and angers that call for rights. They want some voice in choosing their governments and in consenting to the laws that will define their rights. This change also disturbs the waters where humanity must navigate.

There are bound to be true prophets and false prophets; true roads toward freedom and false trails leading into slavery. There is progress toward the real future of useful science, political democracy, and decent human relations, and there are misguided doctrines that lead to tyranny and cruelty. All these rolling seas of hope and fear are part of the great discoveries and hopes of humanity. They may be more than all the resources of human wisdom and good will can master. Our race, and with it all living things on earth, may be doomed to die for our failure to control the fearful forces that we have uncovered. But the Atomic Age has gone on year after year without the sound of the last trumpet, while in the committee rooms of the United Nations men struggle and search for the way to chain the deadly forces and stave off the doom. Every year, while the instruments of destruction grow more deadly, the knowledge of the danger and the determination to avoid it take a sterner hold upon all the governments of the world.

Never, so long as civilization endures on earth, can the human race forget the knowledge that the power of the atom offers a weapon for insane hatred—whether of nations, races, religions, or other divisions of humanity—to destroy all life on earth. The more widely the technical knowledge of that infernal power spreads, the more vital the necessity to create and maintain a spirit of peace and good will. More and more it will be clear that to hate and to organize hatred is to call for universal death.

To this the advance of human thinking has brought us. We and our grandchildren will no doubt do wrong in many ways and yet live, but this one thing we must no longer do. We must not yield ourselves to organized hate. If we can build a world of good will, life can go on so long as our descendants never forget to cherish good will. Beyond that, there is no future.

Haile Selassie I, Emperor of Ethiopia, witnessed the death of the League of Nations after it had failed to respond to his appeal for help in 1936, when Mussolini invaded Ethiopia. He lived to see the defeat of Italy and the founding the United Nations, with Ethiopia as a charter member. On the 4th of October, 1963, he addressed the General Assembly, calling for a further expansion of the peace-keeping powers of the United Nations. At the end of his address he said:

"We must become something we have never been and for which our education and experience and environment have ill prepared us. We must become bigger than we have ever been: more courageous, greater in spirit, larger in outlook: we must become members of a new race, overcoming petty prejudice, owing our ultimate allegiance not to nations but to our fellow men within the human community."

The coming generations, if there are to be any, will work out ways of maintaining peace that will go far beyond our present imaginations. But for our time at least, if there is any hope of avoiding the end of the world, and if there is any way that the human race can ride out the great revolutions of our days and live, those ways are most likely to be found in the slow, painful, but determined labors of the United Nations of the world.

APPENDIX A

Structure of the United Nations and List of Related Intergovernmental Organizations

1. PRINCIPAL ORGANS OF THE UNITED NATIONS

(A) THE GENERAL ASSEMBLY

Main Committees
>First Committee—Political and Security
>Special Political Committee (to assist the First Committee)
>Second Committee—Economic and Financial
>Third Committee—Social, Humanitarian, and Cultural
>Fourth Committee—Trusteeship (including Non-Self-Governing Territories)
>Fifth Committee—Administrative and Budgetary
>Sixth Committee—Legal

Procedural Committees
>Credentials Committee
>General Committee

Standing Committees
>Advisory Committee on Administrative and Budgetary Questions
>Committee on Contributions

Subsidiary and Ad Hoc Bodies
>Disarmament Commission
>UN Scientific Advisory Committee
>Scientific Committee on the Effects of Atomic Radiation
>Committee on the Peaceful Uses of Outer Space
>Peace Observation Commission
>Collective Measures Committee
>Panel for Inquiry and Conciliation

United Nations Relief and Works Agency for Palestine Refugees in the Near East (UNRWA)

UNRWA Advisory Commission

United Nations Conciliation Commission for Palestine

United Nations Commission for the Unification and Rehabilitation of Korea (UNCURK)

United Nations Representative on Hungary

Committee on Arrangements for a Conference for the Purpose of Reviewing the Charter

Interim Committee of the General Assembly

Committee on South West Africa

Ad Hoc Commission on Prisoners of War

Administrator for Residual Affairs of the UN Korean Reconstruction Agency (UNKRA)

UN Commission to Investigate Conditions for Free Elections in Germany

United Nations Emergency Force (UNEF)

Advisory Committee on UNEF

UN Commission on Permanent Sovereignty over Natural Resources

UN Special Fund

Governing Council of the Special Fund

UN High Commissioner for Refugees

Executive Committee of the Program of the UN High Commissioner for Refugees

Committee on Information from Non-Self-Governing Territories

Special Committee to Study the Principles Which Should Guide Members in Determining Whether or Not an Obligation Exists to Transmit Information Under Article 73 (e)

Subcommittee on the Questionnaire (on Trust Territories)

UN Commissioner for the Supervision of the Plebiscite in the Cameroons under United Kingdom Administration

Board of Auditors

Investments Committee

Negotiating Committee for Extra-Budgetary Funds

UN Administrative Tribunal

Committee on Applications for Review of Administrative Tribunal Judgments

Committee of Experts on the Review of the Activities and Organization of the Secretariat

Committee for the United Nations Memorial Cemetery in Korea

United Nations Staff Pension Committee

Expert Group on the Comprehensive Review of the Pension Fund

Consultative Panel on UN Information Policies and Program
International Law Commission
Committee Established under General Assembly Resolution 1181 (XII)—(Question of Defining Aggression)

(B) THE SECURITY COUNCIL
Military Staff Committee

Standing Committees
Committee of Experts
Committee on the Admission of New Members (to the United Nations)

Ad Hoc Bodies
United Nations Commission for Indonesia (adjourned sine die)
United Nations Military Observer Group for India and Pakistan
United Nations Representative for India and Pakistan
United Nations Truce Supervision Organization in Palestine (UNTSO)

(C) ECONOMIC AND SOCIAL COUNCIL
Functional Commissions and Subcommissions
Commission on Human Rights
Subcommission on Prevention of Discrimination and Protection of Minorities
Commission on International Commodity Trade
Commission on Narcotic Drugs
Commission on the Status of Women
Population Commission
Special Commission
Statistical Commission

Regional Economic Commissions
Economic Commission for Africa (ECA)
Economic Commission for Asia and the Far East (ECAFE)
Economic Commission for Europe (ECE)
Economic Commission for Latin America (ECLA)

Standing Committees
Council Committee on Non-Governmental Organizations
Interim Committee on Program of Conferences
Standing Committee for Industrial Development
Technical Assistance Committee (TAC)

Ad Hoc Committees
> Advisory Committee on the Work Program on Industrialization
> Committee of Experts for Further Work on the Transport of Dangerous Goods
> Committee on Program Appraisals (on economic, social, and human rights programs of the UN and related intergovernmental organizations)
> Coordination Committee (on coordination among the UN and related intergovernmental organizations)
> Economic Committee
> Social Committee

Other Bodies reporting to the Council
> Drug Supervisory Body (on narcotic drugs)
> Permanent Central Opium Board (on narcotic drugs)
> United Nations Children's Fund (UNICEF) (established by the General Assembly)
> Executive Board of UNICEF

(D) THE TRUSTEESHIP COUNCIL
Standing Committees
> Standing Committee on Administrative Unions
> Standing Committee on Petitions

Ad Hoc Committees
> Ad Hoc Committee on the Basic Questionnaire
> Committee on Classification of Communications
> Committee on Rural Economic Development of the Trust Territories

(E) THE INTERNATIONAL COURT OF JUSTICE
> Chamber of Summary Procedure

(F) THE SECRETARIAT
Offices of the Secretary-General
> Executive Office of the Secretary-General
> Office of Legal Affairs
> Office of the Controller
> Office of Personnel
> Offices of the Under-Secretaries for Special Political Affairs

Other Departments and Offices
> Department of Political and Security Council Affairs
> Department of Economic and Social Affairs
> Department of Trusteeship and Information from Non-Self-Governing Territories
> Office of Public Information

Office of Conference Services
Office of General Services

II. INTERGOVERNMENTAL ORGANIZATIONS RELATED TO THE UNITED NATIONS

International Atomic Energy Agency (IAEA)
International Labor Organization (ILO)
Food and Agriculture Organization (FAO)
United Nations Educational, Scientific, and Cultural
   Organization (UNESCO)
International Civil Aviation Organization (ICAO)
World Health Organization (WHO)
International Bank for Reconstruction and Development (Bank)
International Finance Corporation (IFC)
International Monetary Fund (Fund)
Universal Postal Union (UPU)
International Telecommunication Union (ITU)
World Meteorological Organization (WMO)
Intergovernmental Maritime Consultative Organization
   (IMCO)

The Contracting Parties to the General Agreement on Tariffs and Trade (GATT) are affiliated with the UN through the GATT Secretariat, which was originally established to serve as the Secretariat for the Interim Commission for the proposed International Trade Organization (ITO). A permanent Organization for Trade Cooperation (OTC) to administer GATT was projected in a 1955 agreement not yet in force.

III. INTERAGENCY BODIES

Administrative Committee on Coordination (ACC)
Panel of External Auditors
Technical Assistance Board (TAB)
Consultative Committee on Public Information
Interim Coordinating Committee for International Commodity Arrangements (ICCICA)
   (reports to the United Nations Economic and
      Social Council)
United Nations Joint Staff Pension Board

APPENDIX B

Charter of the United Nations

SIGNED AT THE UNITED NATIONS CONFERENCE
ON INTERNATIONAL ORGANIZATION,
SAN FRANCISCO, CALIFORNIA, ON JUNE 26, 1945

WE THE PEOPLES OF THE UNITED NATIONS DETERMINED

to save succeeding generations from the scourge of war, which twice in our lifetime has brought untold sorrow to mankind, and

to reaffirm faith in fundamental human rights, in the dignity and worth of the human person, in the equal rights of men and women and of nations large and small, and

to establish conditions under which justice and respect for the obligations arising from treaties and other sources of international law can be maintained, and

to promote social progress and better standards of life in larger freedom,

AND FOR THESE ENDS

to practice tolerance and live together in peace with one another as good neighbors, and

to unite our strength to maintain international peace and security, and

to ensure, by the acceptance of principles and the institution of methods, that armed force shall not be used, save in the common interest, and

to employ international machinery for the promotion of the economic and social advancement of all peoples,

HAVE RESOLVED TO COMBINE OUR EFFORTS TO ACCOMPLISH THESE AIMS.

Accordingly, our respective Governments, through representatives assembled in the city of San Francisco, who have exhibited their full powers found to be in good and due form, have agreed to the present Charter of the United Nations and do hereby establish an international organization to be known as the United Nations.

CHAPTER I

PURPOSES AND PRINCIPLES

Article 1

The Purposes of the United Nations are:

1. To maintain international peace and security, and to that end: to take effective collective measures for the prevention and removal of threats to the peace, and for the suppression of acts of aggression or other breaches of the peace, and to bring about by peaceful means, and in conformity with the principles of justice and international law, adjustment or settlement of international disputes or situations which might lead to a breach of the peace;

2. To develop friendly relations among nations based on respect for the principle of equal rights and self-determination of peoples, and to take other appropriate measures to strengthen universal peace;

3. To achieve international cooperation in solving international problems of an economic, social, cultural, or humanitarian character, and in promoting and encouraging respect for human rights and for fundamental freedoms for all without distinction as to race, sex, language, or religion; and

4. To be a center for harmonizing the actions of nations in the attainment of these common ends.

Article 2

The Organization and its Members, in pursuit of the Purposes stated in Article 1, shall act in accordance with the following Principles.

1. The Organization is based on the principle of the sovereign equality of all its Members.

2. All Members, in order to ensure to all of them the rights and benefits resulting from membership, shall fulfil in good faith the obligations assumed by them in accordance with the present Charter.

3. All Members shall settle their international disputes by peaceful means in such a manner that international peace and security, and justice, are not endangered.

4. All Members shall refrain in their international relations from the threat or use of force against the territorial integrity or political independence of any state, or in any other manner inconsistent with the Purposes of the United Nations.

5. All Members shall give the United Nations every assistance in any action it takes in accordance with the present Charter, and shall refrain from giving assistance to any state against which the United Nations is taking preventive or enforcement action.

6. The Organization shall ensure that states which are not Members of the United Nations act in accordance with these Principles so far as may be necessary for the maintenance of international peace and security.

7. Nothing contained in the present Charter shall authorize the United Nations to intervene in matters which are essentially within the domestic jurisdiction of any state or shall require the Members to submit such matters to settlement under the present Charter; but this principle shall not prejudice the application of enforcement measures under Chapter VII.

CHAPTER II

MEMBERSHIP

Article 3

The original Members of the United Nations shall be the states which, having participated in the United Nations Conference on International Organization at San Francisco, or having previously signed the Declaration by United Nations of January 1, 1942, sign the present Charter and ratify it in accordance with Article 110.

Article 4

1. Membership in the United Nations is open to all other peace-loving states which accept the obligations contained in

the present Charter and, in the judgment of the Organization, are able and willing to carry out these obligations.

2. The admission of any such state to membership in the United Nations will be effected by a decision of the General Assembly upon the recommendation of the Security Council.

Article 5

A Member of the United Nations against which preventive or enforcement action has been taken by the Security Council may be suspended from the exercise of the rights and privileges of membership by the General Assembly upon the recommendation of the Security Council. The exercise of these rights and privileges may be restored by the Security Council.

Article 6

A Member of the United Nations which has persistently violated the Principles contained in the present Charter may be expelled from the Organization by the General Assembly upon the recommendation of the Security Council.

CHAPTER III

ORGANS

Article 7

1. There are established as the principal organs of the United Nations; a General Assembly, a Security Council, an Economic and Social Council, a Trusteeship Council, an International Court of Justice, and a Secretariat.

2. Such subsidiary organs as may be found necessary may be established in accordance with the present Charter.

Article 8

The United Nations shall place no restrictions on the eligibility of men and women to participate in any capacity and under conditions of equality in its principal and subsidiary organs.

CHAPTER IV

THE GENERAL ASSEMBLY

Composition

Article 9

1. The General Assembly shall consist of all the Members of the United Nations.
2. Each Member shall have not more than five representatives in the General Assembly.

Functions and Powers

Article 10

The General Assembly may discuss any questions or any matters within the scope of the present Charter or relating to the powers and functions of any organs provided for in the present Charter, and, except as provided in Article 12, may make recommendations to the Members of the United Nations or to the Security Council or to both on any such questions or matters.

Article 11

1. The General Assembly may consider the general principles of cooperation in the maintenance of international peace and security, including the principles governing disarmament and the regulation of armaments, and may make recommendations with regard to such principles to the Members or to the Security Council or to both.
2. The General Assembly may discuss any questions relating to the maintenance of international peace and security brought before it by any Member of the United Nations, or by the Security Council, or by a state which is not a Member of the United Nations in accordance with Article 35, paragraph 2, and, except as provided in Article 12, may make recommendations with regard to any such questions to the state or states concerned or to the Security Council or to both. Any such question on which action is necessary shall be referred to the Security Council by the General Assembly either before or after discussion.
3. The General Assembly may call the attention of the Security Council to situations which are likely to endanger international peace and security.

4. The powers of the General Assembly set forth in this Article shall not limit the general scope of Article 10.

Article 12

1. While the Security Council is exercising in respect of any dispute or situation the functions assigned to it in the present Charter, the General Assembly shall not make any recommendation with regard to that dispute or situation unless the Security Council so requests.

2. The Secretary-General, with the consent of the Security Council, shall notify the General Assembly at each session of any matters relative to the maintenance of international peace and security which are being dealt with by the Security Council and shall similarly notify the General Assembly, or the Members of the United Nations if the General Assembly is not in session, immediately the Security Council ceases to deal with such matters.

Article 13

1. The General Assembly shall initiate studies and make recommendations for the purpose of:

a. promoting international cooperation in the political field and encouraging the progressive development of international law and its codification;

b. promoting international cooperation in the economic, social, cultural, educational, and health fields, and assisting in the realization of human rights and fundamental freedoms for all without distinction as to race, sex, language, or religion.

2. The further responsibilities, functions and powers of the General Assembly with respect to matters mentioned in paragraph 1 (b) above are set forth in Chapters IX and X.

Article 14

Subject to the provisions of Article 12, the General Assembly may recommend measures for the peaceful adjustment of any situation, regardless of origin, which it deems likely to impair the general welfare or friendly relations among nations, including situations resulting from a violation of the provisions of the present Charter setting forth the Purposes and Principles of the United Nations.

Article 15

1. The General Assembly shall receive and consider annual and special reports from the Security Council; these reports shall include an account of the measures that the Security Council has decided upon or taken to maintain international peace and security.

2. The General Assembly shall receive and consider reports from the other organs of the United Nations.

Article 16

The General Assembly shall perform such functions with respect to the international trusteeship system as are assigned to it under Chapters XII and XIII, including the approval of the trusteeship agreements for areas not designated as strategic.

Article 17

1. The General Assembly shall consider and approve the budget of the Organization.

2. The expenses of the Organization shall be borne by the Members as apportioned by the General Assembly.

3. The General Assembly shall consider and approve any financial and budgetary arrangements with specialized agencies referred to in Article 57 and shall examine the administrative budgets of such specialized agencies with a view to making recommendations to the agencies concerned.

Voting

Article 18

1. Each Member of the General Assembly shall have one vote.

2. Decisions of the General Assembly on important questions shall be made by a two-thirds majority of the Members present and voting. These questions shall include: recommendations with respect to the maintenance of international peace and security, the election of the non-permanent Members of the Security Council, the election of the Members of the Economic and Social Council, the election of Members of the Trusteeship Council in accordance with paragraph 1 (c) of Article 86, the admission of new Members to the United Nations, the suspension of the rights and privileges of membership, the expulsion of Members, questions relating to the

operation of the trusteeship system, and budgetary questions.

3. Decisions on other questions, including the determination of additional categories of questions to be decided by a two-thirds majority, shall be made by a majority of the Members present and voting.

Article 19

A Member of the United Nations which is in arrears in the payment of its financial contributions to the Organization shall have no vote in the General Assembly if the amount of its arrears equals or exceeds the amount of the contributions due from it for the preceding two full years. The General Assembly may, nevertheless, permit such a Member to vote if it is satisfied that the failure to pay is due to conditions beyond the control of the Member.

Procedure

Article 20

The General Assembly shall meet in regular annual sessions and in such special sessions as occasion may require. Special sessions shall be convoked by the Secretary-General at the request of the Security Council or of a majority of the Members of the United Nations.

Article 21

The General Assembly shall adopt its own rules of procedure. It shall elect its President for each session.

Article 22

The General Assembly may establish such subsidiary organs as it deems necessary for the performance of its functions.

CHAPTER V

THE SECURITY COUNCIL

Composition

Article 23

1. The Security Council shall consist of eleven Members of the United Nations. The Republic of China, France, the

Union of Soviet Socialist Republics, the United Kingdom of Great Britain and Northern Ireland, and the United States of America shall be permanent members of the Security Council. The General Assembly shall elect six other Members of the United Nations to be non-permanent members of the Security Council, due regard being specially paid, in the first instance to the contribution of Members of the United Nations to the maintenance of international peace and security and to the other purposes of the Organization, and also to equitable geographical distribution.

2. The non-permanent members of the Security Council shall be elected for a term of two years. In the first election of the non-permanent members, however, three shall be chosen for a term of one year. A retiring member shall not be eligible for immediate re-election.

3. Each member of the Security Council shall have one representative.

Functions and powers

Article 24

1. In order to ensure prompt and effective action by the United Nations, its Members confer on the Security Council primary responsibility for the maintenance of international peace and security, and agree that in carrying out its duties under this responsibility the Security Council acts on their behalf.

2. In discharging these duties the Security Council shall act in accordance with the Purposes and Principles of the United Nations. The specific powers granted to the Security Council for the discharge of these duties are laid down in Chapters VI, VII, VIII, and XII.

3. The Security Council shall submit annual and, when necessary, special reports to the General Assembly for its consideration.

Article 25

The Members of the United Nations agree to accept and carry out the decisions of the Security Council in accordance with the present Charter.

Article 26

In order to promote the establishment and maintenance of international peace and security with the least diversion for armaments of the world's human and economic resources, the

Security Council shall be responsible for formulating, with the assistance of the Military Staff Committee referred to in Article 47, plans to be submitted to the Members of the United Nations for the establishment of a system for the regulation of armaments.

Voting

Article 27

1. Each member of the Security Council shall have one vote.

2. Decisions of the Security Council on procedural matters shall be made by an affirmative vote of seven members.

3. Decisions of the Security Council on all other matters shall be made by an affirmative vote of seven members, including the concurring votes of the permanent members; provided that, in decisions under Chapter VI, and under paragraph 3 of Article 52, a party to a dispute shall abstain from voting.

Procedure

Article 28

1. The Security Council shall be so organized as to be able to function continuously. Each member of the Security Council shall for this purpose be represented at all times at the seat of the Organization.

2. The Security Council shall hold periodic meetings at which each of its members may, if it so desires, be represented by a member of the government or by some other specially designated representative.

3. The Security Council may hold meetings at such places other than the seat of the Organization as in its judgment will best facilitate its work.

Article 29

The Security Council may establish such subsidiary organs as it deems necessary for the performance of its functions.

Article 30

The Security Council shall adopt its own rules of procedure, including the method of selecting its President.

Article 31

Any Member of the United Nations which is not a member of the Security Council may participate, without vote, in the discussion of any question brought before the Security Council whenever the latter considers that the interests of that Member are specially affected.

Article 32

Any Member of the United Nations which is not a member of the Security Council or any state which is not a Member of the United Nations, if it is a party to a dispute under consideration by the Security Council, shall be invited to participate, without vote, in the discussion relating to the dispute. The Security Council shall lay down such conditions as it deems just for the participation of a state which is not a Member of the United Nations.

CHAPTER VI

PACIFIC SETTLEMENT OF DISPUTES

Article 33

1. The parties to any dispute, the continuance of which is likely to endanger the maintenance of international peace and security, shall, first of all, seek a solution by negotiation, enquiry, mediation, conciliation, arbitration, judicial settlement, resort to regional agencies or arrangements, or other peaceful means of their own choice.
2. The Security Council shall, when it deems necessary, call upon the parties to settle their dispute by such means.

Article 34

The Security Council may investigate any dispute, or any situation which might lead to international friction or give rise to a dispute, in order to determine whether the continuance of the dispute or situation is likely to endanger the maintenance of international peace and security.

Article 35

1. Any Member of the United Nations may bring any dispute, or any situation of the nature referred to in Article 34,

to the attention of the Security Council or of the General Assembly.

2. A state which is not a Member of the United Nations may bring to the attention of the Security Council or of the General Assembly any dispute to which it is a party if it accepts in advance, for the purpose of the dispute, the obligations of pacific settlement provided in the present Charter.

3. The proceedings of the General Assembly in respect of matters brought to its attention under this Article will be subject to the provisions of Articles 11 and 12.

Article 36

1. The Security Council may, at any stage of a dispute of the nature referred to in Article 33 or of a situation of like nature, recommend appropriate procedures or methods of adjustment.

2. The Security Council should take into consideration any procedures for the settlement of the dispute which have already been adopted by the parties.

3. In making recommendations under this Article the Security Council should also take into consideration that legal disputes should as a general rule be referred by the parties to the International Court of Justice in accordance with the provisions of the Statute of the Court.

Article 37

1. Should the parties to a dispute of the nature referred to in Article 33 fail to settle it by the means indicated in that Article, they shall refer it to the Security Council.

2. If the Security Council deems that the continuance of the dispute is in fact likely to endanger the maintenance of international peace and security, it shall decide whether to take action under Article 36 or to recommend such terms of settlement as it may consider appropriate.

Article 38

Without prejudice to the provisions of Articles 33 to 37, the Security Council may, if all the parties to any dispute so request, make recommendations to the parties with a view to a pacific settlement of the dispute.

CHAPTER VII

ACTION WITH RESPECT TO THREATS TO THE
PEACE, BREACHES OF THE PEACE,
AND ACTS OF AGGRESSION

Article 39

The Security Council shall determine the existence of any threat to the peace, breach of the peace, or act of aggression and shall make recommendations, or decide what measures shall be taken in accordance with Articles 41 and 42, to maintain or restore international peace and security.

Article 40

In order to prevent an aggravation of the situation, the Security Council may, before making the recommendations or deciding upon the measures provided for in Article 39, call upon the parties concerned to comply with such provisional measures as it deems necessary or desirable. Such provisional measures shall be without prejudice to the rights, claims, or position of the parties concerned. The Security Council shall duly take account of failure to comply with such provisional measures.

Article 41

The Security Council may decide what measures not in- volving the use of armed force are to be employed to give effect to its decisions, and it may call upon the Members of the United Nations to apply such measures. These may in- clude complete or partial interruption of economic relations and of rail, sea, air, postal, telegraphic, radio, and other means of communication, and the severance of diplomatic relations.

Article 42

Should the Security Council consider that measures pro- vided for in Article 41 would be inadequate or have proved to be inadequate, it may take such action by air, sea, or land forces as may be necessary to maintain or restore inter- national peace and security. Such action may include demon- strations, blockade, and other operations by air, sea, or land forces of Members of the United Nations.

Article 43

1. All Members of the United Nations, in order to contribute to the maintenance of international peace and security, undertake to make available to the Security Council, on its call and in accordance with a special agreement or agreements, armed forces, assistance and facilities, including rights of passage, necessary for the purpose of maintaining international peace and security.

2. Such agreement or agreements shall govern the numbers and types of forces, their degree of readiness and general location, and the nature of the facilities and assistance to be provided.

3. The agreement or agreements shall be negotiated as soon as possible on the initiative of the Security Council. They shall be concluded between the Security Council and Members or between the Security Council and groups of Members and shall be subject to ratification by the signatory states in accordance with their respective constitutional processes.

Article 44

When the Security Council has decided to use force it shall, before calling upon a Member not represented on it to provide armed forces in fulfilment of the obligations assumed under Article 43, invite that Member, if the Member so desires, to participate in the decisions of the Security Council concerning the employment of contingents of that Member's armed forces.

Article 45

In order to enable the United Nations to take urgent military measures, Members shall hold immediately available national air-force contingents for combined international enforcement action. The strength and degree of readiness of these contingents and plans for their combined action shall be determined, within the limits laid down in the special agreement or agreements referred to in Article 43, by the Security Council with the assistance of the Military Staff Committee.

Article 46

Plans for the application of armed force shall be made by the Security Council with the assistance of the Military Staff

Committee.

Article 47

1. There shall be established a Military Staff Committee to advise and assist the Security Council on all questions relating to the Security Council's military requirements for the maintenance of international peace and security, the employment and command of forces placed at its disposal, the regulation of armaments, and possible disarmament.

2. The Military Staff Committee shall consist of the Chiefs of Staff of the permanent members of the Security Council or their representatives. Any Member of the United Nations not permanently represented on the Committee shall be invited by the Committee to be associated with it when the efficient discharge of the Committee's responsibilities requires the participation of that Member in its work.

3. The Military Staff Committee shall be responsible under the Security Council for the strategic direction of any armed forces placed at the disposal of the Security Council. Questions relating to the command of such forces shall be worked out subsequently.

4. The Military Staff Committee, with the authorization of the Security Council and after consultation with appropriate regional agencies, may establish regional subcommittees.

Article 48

1. The action required to carry out the decisions of the Security Council for the maintenance of international peace and security shall be taken by all the Members of the United Nations or by some of them, as the Security Council may determine.

2. Such decisions shall be carried out by the Members of the United Nations directly and through their action in the appropriate international agencies of which they are members.

Article 49

The Members of the United Nations shall join in affording mutual assistance in carrying out the measures decided upon by the Security Council.

Article 50

If preventive or enforcement measures against any state are taken by the Security Council, any other state, whether a Member of the United Nations or not, which finds itself confronted with special economic problems arising from the carrying out of those measures shall have the right to consult the Security Council with regard to a solution of those problems.

Article 51

Nothing in the present Charter shall impair the inherent right of individual or collective self-defense if an armed attack occurs against a Member of the United Nations, until the Security Council has taken measures necessary to maintain international peace and security. Measures taken by Members in the exercise of this right of self-defense shall be immediately reported to the Security Council and shall not in any way affect the authority and responsibility of the Security Council under the present Charter to take at any time such action as it deems necessary in order to maintain or restore international peace and security.

CHAPTER VIII

REGIONAL ARRANGEMENTS

Article 52

1. Nothing in the present Charter precludes the existence of regional arrangements or agencies for dealing with such matters relating to the maintenance of international peace and security as are appropriate for regional action, provided that such arrangements or agencies and their activities are consistent with the Purposes and Principles of the United Nations.

2. The Members of the United Nations entering into such arrangements or constituting such agencies shall make every effort to achieve pacific settlement of local disputes through such regional arrangements or by such regional agencies before referring them to the Security Council.

3. The Security Council shall encourage the development of pacific settlement of local disputes through such regional arrangements or by such regional agencies either on the initiative of the states concerned or by reference from the Security Council.

4. This Article in no way impairs the application of Articles 34 and 35.

Article 53

1. The Security Council shall, where appropriate, utilize such regional arrangements or agencies for enforcement ac-

tion under its authority. But no enforcement action shall be taken under regional arrangements or by regional agencies

without the authorization of the Security Council, with the exception of measures against any enemy state, as defined in paragraph 2 of this Article, provided for pursuant to Article 107 or in regional arrangements directed against renewal of aggressive policy on the part of any such state, until such time as the Organization may, on request of the Governments concerned, be charged with the responsibility for preventing further aggression by such a state.

2. The term enemy state as used in paragraph 1 of this Article applies to any state which during the Second World War has been an enemy of any signatory of the present Charter.

Article 54

The Security Council shall at all times be kept fully informed of activities undertaken or in contemplation under regional arrangements or by regional agencies for the maintenance of international peace and security.

CHAPTER IX

INTERNATIONAL ECONOMIC AND SOCIAL COOPERATION

Article 55

With a view to the creation of conditions of stability and well-being which are necessary for peaceful and friendly relations among nations based on respect for the principle of equal rights and self-determination of peoples, the United Nations shall promote:

a. higher standards of living, full employment, and conditions of economic and social progress and development;

b. solutions of international economic, social, health, and related problems; and international cultural and educational cooperation; and

c. universal respect for, and observance of, human rights and fundamental freedoms for all without distinction as to race, sex, language, or religion.

Article 56

All Members pledge themselves to take joint and separate action in cooperation with the Organization for the achievement of the purposes set forth in Article 55.

Article 57

1. The various specialized agencies, established by intergovernmental agreement and having wide international responsibilities, as defined in their basic instruments, in economic, social, cultural, educational, health, and related fields, shall be brought into relationship with the United Nations in accordance with the provisions of Article 63.
2. Such agencies thus brought into relationship with the United Nations are hereinafter referred to as specialized agencies.

Article 58

The Organization shall make recommendations for the coordination of the policies and activities of the specialized agencies.

Article 59

The Organization shall, where appropriate, initiate negotiations among the states concerned for the creation of any new specialized agencies required for the accomplishment of the purposes set forth in Article 55.

Article 60

Responsibility for the discharge of the functions of the Organization set forth in this Chapter shall be vested in the General Assembly and, under the authority of the General Assembly, in the Economic and Social Council, which shall have for this purpose the powers set forth in Chapter X.

CHAPTER X

THE ECONOMIC AND SOCIAL COUNCIL

Composition

Article 61

1. The Economic and Social Council shall consist of eighteen Members of the United Nations elected by the General Assembly.

2. Subject to the provisions of paragraph 3, six members of the Economic and Social Council shall be elected each year for a term of three years. A retiring member shall be eligible for immediate re-election.

3. At the first election, eighteen members of the Economic and Social Council shall be chosen. The term of office of six members so chosen shall expire at the end of one year, and of six other members at the end of two years, in accordance with arrangements made by the General Assembly.

4. Each member of the Economic and Social Council shall have one representative.

Functions and Powers

Article 62

1. The Economic and Social Council may make or initiate studies and reports with respect to international economic, social, cultural, educational, health, and related matters and may make recommendations with respect to any such matters to the General Assembly, to the Members of the United Nations, and to the specialized agencies concerned.

2. It may make recommendations for the purpose of promoting respect for, and observance of, human rights and fundamental freedoms for all.

3. It may prepare draft conventions for submission to the General Assembly, with respect to matters falling within its competence.

4. It may call, in accordance with the rules prescribed by the United Nations, international conferences on matters falling within its competence.

Article 63

1. The Economic and Social Council may enter into agreements with any of the agencies referred to in Article 57, defining the terms on which the agency concerned shall be

brought into relationship with the United Nations. Such agreements shall be subject to approval by the General Assembly.

2. It may coordinate the activities of the specialized agencies through consultation with and recommendations to such agencies and through recommendations to the General Assembly and to the Members of the United Nations.

Article 64

1. The Economic and Social Council may take appropriate steps to obtain regular reports from the specialized agencies. It may make arrangements with the Members of the United Nations and with the specialized agencies to obtain reports on the steps taken to give effect to its own recommendations and to recommendations on matters falling within its competence made by the General Assembly.

2. It may communicate its observations on these reports to the General Assembly.

Article 65

The Economic and Social Council may furnish information to the Security Council and shall assist the Security Council upon its request.

Article 66

1. The Economic and Social Council shall perform such functions as fall within its competence in connection with the carrying out of the recommendations of the General Assembly.

2. It may, with the approval of the General Assembly, perform services at the request of Members of the United Nations and at the request of specialized agencies.

3. It shall perform such other functions as are specified elsewhere in the present Charter or as may be assigned to it by the General Assembly.

Voting

Article 67

1. Each member of the Economic and Social Council shall have one vote.

2. Decisions of the Economic and Social Council shall be made by a majority of the members present and voting.

Procedure

Article 68

The Economic and Social Council shall set up commissions in economic and social fields and for the promotion of human rights, and such other commissions as may be required for the performance of its functions.

Article 69

The Economic and Social Council shall invite any Member of the United Nations to participate, without vote, in its deliberations on any matter of particular concern to that Member.

Article 70

The Economic and Social Council may make arrangements for representatives of the specialized agencies to participate, without vote, in its deliberations and in those of the commissions established by it, and for its representatives to participate in the deliberations of the specialized agencies.

Article 71

The Economic and Social Council may make suitable arrangements for consultation with non-governmental organizations which are concerned with matters within its competence. Such arrangements may be made with international organizations and, where appropriate, with national organizations after consultation with the Member of the United Nations concerned.

Article 72

1. The Economic and Social Council shall adopt its own rules of procedure, including the method of selecting its President.
2. The Economic and Social Council shall meet as required in accordance with its rules, which shall include provision for the convening of meetings on the request of a majority of its members.

CHAPTER XI

DECLARATION REGARDING
NON-SELF-GOVERNING TERRITORIES

Article 73

Members of the United Nations which have or assume responsibilities for the administration of territories whose peoples have not yet attained a full measure of self-government recognize the principle that the interests of the inhabitants of these territories are paramount, and accept as a sacred trust the obligation to promote to the utmost, within the system of international peace and security established by the present Charter, the well-being of the inhabitants of these territories, and, to this end:

a. to ensure, with due respect for the culture of the peoples concerned, their political, economic, social, and educational advancement, their just treatment, and their protection against abuses;

b. to develop self-government, to take due account of the political aspirations of the peoples, and to assist them in the progressive development of their free political institutions, according to the particular circumstances of each territory and its peoples and their varying stages of advancement;

c. to further international peace and security;

d. to promote constructive measures of development, to encourage research, and to cooperate with one another and, when and where appropriate, with specialized international bodies with a view to the practical achievement of the social, economic, and scientific purposes set forth in this Article; and

e. to transmit regularly to the Secretary-General for information purposes, subject to such limitation as security and constitutional considerations may require, statistical and other information of a technical nature relating to economic, social, and educational conditions in the territories for which they are respectively responsible other than those territories to which Chapters XII and XIII apply.

Article 74

Members of the United Nations also agree that their policy in respect of the territories to which this Chapter applies, no less than in respect of their metropolitan areas, must be based on the general principle of good-neighborliness, due account being taken of the interests and well-being of the rest of the world, in social, economic, and commercial matters.

CHAPTER XII

INTERNATIONAL TRUSTEESHIP SYSTEM

Article 75

The United Nations shall establish under its authority an international trusteeship system for the administration and supervision of such territories as may be placed thereunder by subsequent individual agreements. These territories are hereinafter referred to as trust territories.

Article 76

The basic objectives of the trusteeship system, in accordance with the Purposes of the United Nations laid down in Article 1 of the present Charter, shall be:

a. to further international peace and security;

b. to promote the political, economic, social, and educational advancement of the inhabitants of the trust territories, and their progressive development towards self-government or independence as may be appropriate to the particular circumstances of each territory and its peoples and the freely expressed wishes of the peoples concerned, and as may be provided by the terms of each trusteeship agreement;

c. to encourage respect for human rights and for fundamental freedoms for all without distinction as to race, sex, language, or religion, and to encourage recognition of the interdependence of the peoples of the world; and

d. to ensure equal treatment in social, economic, and commercial matters for all Members of the United Nations and their nationals, and also equal treatment for the latter in the administration of justice, without prejudice to the attainment of the foregoing objectives and subject to the provisions of Article 80.

Article 77

1. The trusteeship system shall apply to such territories in the following categories as may be placed thereunder by means of trusteeship agreements:

a. territories now held under mandate;

b. territories which may be detached from enemy states as a result of the Second World War; and

c. territories voluntarily placed under the system by states responsible for their administration.

2. It will be a matter for subsequent agreement as to which territories in the foregoing categories will be brought under the trusteeship system and upon what terms.

Article 78

The trusteeship system shall not apply to territories which have become Members of the United Nations, relationship among which shall be based on respect for the principle of sovereign equality.

Article 79

The terms of trusteeship for each territory to be placed under the trusteeship system, including any alteration or amendment, shall be agreed upon by the states directly concerned, including the mandatory power in the case of territories held under mandate by a Member of the United Nations, and shall be approved as provided for in Articles 83 and 85.

Article 80

1. Except as may be agreed upon in individual trusteeship agreements, made under Articles 77, 79, and 81, placing each territory under the trusteeship system, and until such agreements have been concluded, nothing in this Chapter shall be constructed in or of itself to alter in any manner the rights whatsoever of any states or any peoples or the terms of existing international instruments to which Members of the United Nations may respectively be parties.

2. Paragraph 1 of this Article shall not be interpreted as giving grounds for delay or postponement of the negotiation and conclusion of agreements for placing mandated and other territories under the trusteeship system as provided for in Article 77.

Article 81

The trusteeship agreement shall in each case include the terms under which the trust territory will be administered and designate the authority which will exercise the administration of the trust territory. Such authority, hereinafter called the administering authority, may be one or more states or the Organization itself.

Article 82

There may be designated, in any trusteeship agreement, a strategic area or areas which may include part or all of the trust territory to which the agreement applies, without prejudice to any special agreement or agreements made under Article 43.

Article 83

1. All functions of the United Nations relating to strategic areas, including the approval of the terms of the trusteeship agreements and of their alteration or amendment, shall be exercised by the Security Council.
2. The basic objectives set forth in Article 76 shall be applicable to the people of each strategic area.
3. The Security Council shall, subject to the provisions of the trusteeship agreements and without prejudice to security considerations, avail itself of the assistance of the Trusteeship Council to perform those functions of the United Nations under the trusteeship system relating to political, economic, social, and educational matters in the strategic areas.

Article 84

It shall be the duty of the administering authority to ensure that the trust territory shall play its part in the maintenance of international peace and security. To this end the administering authority may make use of volunteer forces, facilities, and assistance from the trust territory in carrying out the obligations towards the Security Council undertaken in this regard by the administering authority, as well as for local defense and the maintenance of law and order within the trust territory.

Article 85

1. The functions of the United Nations with regard to trusteeship agreements for all areas not designated as strategic, including the approval of the terms of the trusteeship agreements and of their alteration or amendment, shall be exercised by the General Assembly.
2. The Trusteeship Council, operating under the authority of the General Assembly, shall assist the General Assembly in carrying out these functions.

CHAPTER XIII

THE TRUSTEESHIP COUNCIL

Composition

Article 86

1. The Trusteeship Council shall consist of the following Members of the United Nations:

  a. those Members administering trust territories;

  b. such of those Members mentioned by name in Article 23 as are not administering trust territories; and

  c. as many other Members elected for three-year terms by the General Assembly as may be necessary to ensure that the total number of members of the Trusteeship Council is equally divided between those Members of the United Nations which administer trust territories and those which do not.

2. Each member of the Trusteeship Council shall designate one specially qualified person to represent it therein.

Functions and Powers

Article 87

The General Assembly and, under its authority, the Trusteeship Council, in carrying out their functions, may:

  a. consider reports submitted by the administering authority;

  b. accept petitions and examine them in consultation with the administering authority;

  c. provide for periodic visits to the respective trust territories at times agreed upon with the administering authority; and

  d. take these and other actions in conformity with the terms of the trusteeship agreements.

Article 88

The Trusteeship Council shall formulate a questionnaire on the political, economic, social, and educational advancement of the inhabitants of each trust territory, and the administering authority for each trust territory, within the competence of the General Assembly, shall make an annual report to the General Assembly upon the basis of such questionnaire.

Voting

Article 89

1. Each member of the Trusteeship Council shall have one vote.
2. Decisions of the Trusteeship Council shall be made by a majority of the members present and voting.

Procedure

Article 90

1. The Trusteeship Council shall adopt its own rules of procedure, including the method of selecting its President.
2. The Trusteeship Council shall meet as required in accordance with its rules, which shall include provision for the convening of meetings on the request of a majority of its members.

Article 91

The Trusteeship Council shall, when appropriate, avail itself of the assistance of the Economic and Social Council and of the specialized agencies in regard to matters with which they are respectively concerned.

CHAPTER XIV

THE INTERNATIONAL COURT OF JUSTICE

Article 92

The International Court of Justice shall be the principal judicial organ of the United Nations. It shall function in accordance with the annexed Statute, which is based upon the Statute of the Permanent Court of International Justice and forms an integral part of the present Charter.

Article 93

1. All Members of the United Nations are *ipso facto* parties to the Statute of the International Court of Justice.
2. A state which is not a Member of the United Nations

may become a party to the Statute of the International Court of Justice on conditions to be determined in each case by the General Assembly upon the recommendation of the Security Council.

Article 94

1. Each Member of the United Nations undertakes to comply with the decision of the International Court of Justice in any case to which it is a party.
2. If any party to a case fails to perform the obligations incumbent upon it under a judgment rendered by the Court, the other party may have recourse to the Security Council, which may, if it deems necessary, make recommendations or decide upon measures to be taken to give effect to the judgment.

Article 95

Nothing in the present Charter shall prevent Members of the United Nations from entrusting the solution of their differences to other tribunals by virtue of agreements already in existence or which may be concluded in the future.

Article 96

1. The General Assembly or the Security Council may request the International Court of Justice to give an advisory opinion on any legal question.
2. Other organs of the United Nations and specialized agencies, which may at any time be so authorized by the General Assembly, may also request advisory opinions of the Court on legal questions arising within the scope of their activities.

CHAPTER XV

THE SECRETARIAT

Article 97

The Secretariat shall comprise a Secretary-General and such staff as the Organization may require. The Secretary-General shall be appointed by the General Assembly upon the recommendation of the Security Council. He shall be the chief administrative officer of the Organization.

Article 98

The Secretary-General shall act in that capacity in all meetings of the General Assembly, of the Security Council, of the Economic and Social Council, and of the Trusteeship Council, and shall perform such other functions as are entrusted to him by these organs. The Secretary-General shall make an annual report to the General Assembly on the work of the Organization.

Article 99

The Secretary-General may bring to the attention of the Security Council any matter which in his opinion may threaten the maintenance of international peace and security.

Article 100

1. In the performance of their duties, the Secretary-General and the staff shall not seek or receive instructions from any government or from any other authority external to the Organization. They shall refrain from any action which might reflect on their position as international officials responsible only to the Organization.

2. Each Member of the United Nations undertakes to respect the exclusively international character of the responsibilities of the Secretary-General and the staff and not to seek to influence them in the discharge of their responsibilities.

Article 101

1. The staff shall be appointed by the Secretary-General under regulations established by the General Assembly.

2. Appropriate staffs shall be permanently assigned to the Economic and Social Council, the Trusteeship Council, and, as required, to other organs of the United Nations. These staffs shall form a part of the Secretariat.

3. The paramount consideration in the employment of the staff and in the determination of the conditions of service shall be the necessity of securing the highest standards of efficiency, competence, and integrity. Due regard shall be paid to the importance of recruiting the staff on as wide a geographical basis as possible.

CHAPTER XVI

MISCELLANEOUS PROVISIONS

Article 102

1. Every treaty and every international agreement entered into by any Member of the United Nations after the present Charter comes into force shall as soon as possible be registered with the Secretariat and published by it.

2. No party to any such treaty or international agreement which has not been registered in accordance with the provisions of paragraph 1 of this Article may invoke that treaty or agreement before any organ of the United Nations.

Article 103

In the event of a conflict between the obligations of the Members of the United Nations under the present Charter and their obligations under any other international agreement, their obligations under the present Charter shall prevail.

Article 104

The Organization shall enjoy in the territory of each of its Members such legal capacity as may be necessary for the exercise of its functions and the fulfilment of its purposes.

Article 105

1. The Organization shall enjoy in the territory of each of its Members such privileges and immunities as are necessary for the fulfilment of its purposes.

2. Representatives of the Members of the United Nations and officials of the Organization shall similarly enjoy such privileges and immunities as are necessary for the independent exercise of their functions in connection with the Organization.

3. The General Assembly may make recommendations with a view to determining the details of the application of paragraphs 1 and 2 of this Article or may propose conventions to the Members of the United Nations for this purpose.

CHAPTER XVII

TRANSITIONAL SECURITY ARRANGEMENTS

Article 106

Pending the coming into force of such special agreements referred to in Article 43 as in the opinion of the Security Council enable it to begin the exercise of its responsibilities under Article 42, the parties to the Four-Nation Declaration, signed at Moscow, October 30, 1943, and France, shall, in accordance with the provisions of paragraph 5 of that Declaration, consult with one another and as occasion requires with other Members of the United Nations with a view to such joint action on behalf of the Organization as may be neces-

sary for the purpose of maintaining international peace and
security.

Article 107

Nothing in the present Charter shall invalidate or preclude
action, in relation to any state which during the Second
World War has been an enemy of any signatory to the present Charter, taken or authorized as a result of that war by the
Governments having responsibility for such action.

CHAPTER XVIII

AMENDMENTS

Article 108

Amendments to the present Charter shall come into force
for all Members of the United Nations when they have been
adopted by a vote of two thirds of the members of the General Assembly and ratified in accordance with their respective
constitutional processes by two thirds of the Members of the
United Nations, including all the permanent members of
the Security Council.

Article 109

1. A general conference of the Members of the United
Nations for the purpose of reviewing the present Charter may
be held at a date and place to be fixed by a two-thirds vote of
the members of the General Assembly and by a vote of any
seven members of the Security Council. Each Member of
the United Nations shall have one vote in the conference.
2. Any alteration of the present Charter recommended by
a two-thirds vote of the conference shall take effect when
ratified in accordance with their respective constitutional
processes by two thirds of the Members of the United Nations, including all the permanent members of the Security
Council.
3. If such a conference has not been held before the tenth
annual session of the General Assembly following the coming
into force of the present Charter, the proposal to call such a
conference shall be placed on the agenda of that session of
the General Assembly, and the conference shall be held if
so decided by a majority vote of the members of the General
Assembly and by a vote of any seven members of the Security
Council.

CHAPTER XIX

RATIFICATION AND SIGNATURE

Article 110

1. The present Charter shall be ratified by the signatory states in accordance with their respective constitutional processes.

2. The ratifications shall be deposited with the Government of the United States of America, which shall notify all the signatory states of each deposit as well as the Secretary-General of the Organization when he has been appointed.

3. The present Charter shall come into force upon the deposit of ratifications by the Republic of China, France, the Union of Soviet Socialist Republics, the United Kingdom of Great Britain and Northern Ireland, and the United States of America, and by a majority of the other signatory states. A protocol of the ratifications deposited shall thereupon be drawn up by the Government of the United States of America, which shall communicate copies thereof to all the signatory states.

4. The states signatory to the present Charter which ratify it after it has come into force will become original Members of the United Nations on the date of the deposit of their respective ratifications.

Article 111

The present Charter, of which the Chinese, French, Russian, English, and Spanish texts are equally authentic, shall remain deposited in the archives of the Government of the United States of America. Duly certified copies thereof shall be transmitted by that Government to the Governments of the other signatory states.

IN FAITH WHEREOF the representatives of the Governments of the United Nations have signed the present Charter.

DONE at the city of San Francisco the twenty-sixth day of June, one thousand nine hundred and forty-five.

Note: The Statute of the International Court of Justice is an integral part of the Charter of the United Nations. It has been omitted here, however, since, in a book of this size, space for appended material is limited.

APPENDIX C

The 115 member states of the United Nations are:

Afghanistan
Albania
Algeria
*Argentina
*Australia
Austria
*Belgium
*Bolivia
*Brazil
Bulgaria
Burma
Burundi
*Byelorussian SSR
Cambodia
Cameroon
*Canada
Central African
    Republic
Ceylon
Chad
*Chile
*China
*Colombia
Congo (Brazzaville)
Congo, Democratic Re-
    public of
*Costa Rica
*Cuba
Cyprus
*Czechoslovakia
Dahomey
*Denmark
*Dominican Republic

*Ecuador
*El Salvador
*Ethiopia
Finland
*France
Gabon
Ghana
*Greece
*Guatemala
Guinea
*Haiti
*Honduras
Hungary
Iceland
*India
Indonesia
*Iran
*Iraq
Ireland
Israel
Italy
Ivory Coast
Jamaica
Japan
Jordan
Kenya
Kuwait
Laos
*Lebanon
*Liberia
Libya
*Luxembourg
Madagascar

249

** Malawi
Malaysia
Mali
** Malta
Mauritania
*Mexico
Mongolia
Morocco
Nepal
*Netherlands
*New Zealand
*Nicaragua
Niger
Nigeria
*Norway
Pakistan
*Panama
*Paraguay
*Peru
*Philippines
*Poland
Portugal
Romania
Rwanda
*Saudi Arabia
Senegal

Sierra Leone
Somalia
*South Africa
Spain
Sudan
Sweden
Syria
Thailand
Togo
Trinidad and Tobago
Tunisia
*Turkey
Uganda
*Ukrainian SSR
*USSR
***United Arab Republic
*United Kingdom
United Republic of
Tanzania
*United States
Upper Volta
*Uruguay
*Venezuela
Yemen
*Yugoslavia
** Zambia

* Original member.
** At the time this book went to press, January, 1965, these three
additional states had recently been admitted to membership in the
United Nations.
*** In 1958, Egypt and Syria, original members of the United Nations,
were united in a single state, the United Arab Republic. On October 13,
1961, Syria, having resumed its status as an independent state, also resumed separate membership in the UN.

INDEX

251